THE
ELEMENTS
OF
PROGRAMMING
STYLE

THE

ELEMENTS

OF

PROGRAMMING

STYLE

Brian W. Kernighan

P. J. Plauger

Bell Telephone Laboratories, Incorporated
Murray Hill, New Jersey

McGraw-Hill Book Company

New York   St. Louis   San Francisco   Düsseldorf   Johannesburg   Kuala Lumpur
London   Mexico City   Montreal   New Delhi   Panama   Paris   São Paulo
Singapore   Sydney   Tokyo   Toronto

Library of Congress Cataloging in Publication Data

Kernighan, Brian W.
    The elements of programming style.

    Bibliography: p.
    1. Electronic digital computers—Programming.
I. Plauger, P.J., date   joint author.
II. Title.
QA76.6.K47   001.6'42   73-20165
ISBN 0.07-034199-0

The Elements of Programming Style

234567890WHWH7987654

*This book was set in Times Roman and News Gothic Condensed by the
authors, using a Graphic Systems phototypesetter driven by a PDP 11/45
running under the UNIX operating system.*

We are deeply indebted to the following authors and publishers for their kind permission to reproduce excerpts from the following copyrighted material:

R. V. Andree, J. P. Andree, and D. D. Andree, *Computer Programming Techniques, Analysis, and Mathematics.* Copyright © 1973 by R. V. Andree. By permission of Prentice-Hall, Inc.

C. R. Bauer, A. P. Peluso, and D. A. Gomberg, *Basic PL/I Programming.* Copyright © Addison-Wesley Publishing Company, 1968. By permission.

V. J. Calderbank, *A Course on Programming in Fortran IV.* Copyright © Chapman and Hall, Ltd., 1969. By permission.

Frank J. Clark, *Introduction to PL/I Programming.* Copyright © 1971 by Allyn and Bacon, Inc. Used by permission.

D. F. DeTar, *Principles of Fortran Programming.* Copyright © 1972 by W. A. Benjamin, Inc., Menlo Park, California. By permission.

H. Dinter, *Introduction to Computing.* Copyright © 1973, Heinz Dinter. By permission of The Macmillan Company, New York.

D. Dmitry and T. Mott, Jr., *Introduction to Fortran IV Programming.* Copyright © Holt, Rinehart and Winston, Inc., 1966. By permission.

W. S. Dorn, G. G. Bitter, and D. L. Hector, *Computer Applications for Calculus.* Copyright © Prindle, Weber & Schmidt, 1972. By permission.

M. V. Farina, *Fortran IV Self-Taught.* Copyright © Prentice-Hall, Inc., 1966. By permission.

Gabriel F. Groner, *PL/I Programming in Technological Applications.* Copyright © 1971 by John Wiley and Sons, Inc. Reprinted by permission of the publisher.

J. N. Haag, *Comprehensive Standard Fortran Programming.* Copyright © Hayden Book Company, Inc., 1969. By permission.

Malcolm C. Harrison, *Data-Structures and Programming.* Copyright © 1973 by Scott, Foresman and Company. Reprinted by permission of the publisher.

C. B. Kreitzberg and B. Schneiderman, *The Elements of Fortran Style.* Copyright © 1972 by Harcourt Brace Jovanovich, Inc., and reprinted with their permission.

S. S. Kuo, *Computer Applications of Numerical Methods.* Copyright © Addison-Wesley Publishing Company, 1972. By permission.

R. S. Ledley, *Fortran IV Programming.* Copyright © McGraw-Hill, Inc., 1966. By permission.

W. A. Manning and R. S. Garnero, *A Fortran IV Problem Solver.* Copyright © McGraw-Hill, Inc., 1970. By permission.

Mary McCammon, *Understanding Fortran.* Copyright © 1968 by Thomas Y. Crowell Company, Inc.. With permission of the publisher.

D. D. McCracken, *A Guide to Fortran IV Programming.* Copyright © 1965 by John Wiley and Sons, Inc. Reprinted by permission of the publisher.

D. D. McCracken, *A Guide to Fortran IV Programming, Second Edition.* Copyright © 1972 by John Wiley and Sons, Inc. Reprinted by permission of the publisher.

H. Mullish, *Modern Programming: Fortran IV.* Copyright © 1968, Xerox Corporation. All rights reserved. By permission.

R. L. Nolan, *Fortran IV Computing and Applications.* Copyright © Addison-Wesley Publishing Company, 1971. By permission.

S. V. Pollack, *A Guide to Fortran IV.* Copyright © Columbia University Press, 1965. By permission.

S. V. Pollack and T. D. Sterling, *A Guide to PL/I.* Copyright © 1969 by Holt, Rinehart and Winston, Inc. Reprinted by permission of Holt, Rinehart and Winston, Inc.

A. Ralston, *Fortran IV Programming, A Concise Exposition.* Copyright © McGraw-Hill, Inc., 1971. By permission.

J. K. Rice and J. R. Rice, *Introduction to Computer Science.* Copyright © 1969 by Holt, Rinehart and Winston, Inc. Reprinted by permission of Holt, Rinehart and Winston, Inc.

W. P. Rule, *Fortran IV Programming.* Copyright © 1968 W. P. Rule. Prindle, Weber & Schmidt, Incorporated.

School Mathematics Study Group, *Algorithms, Computation and Mathematics, Fortran Supplement, Student Text (Revised Edition).* Copyright © Stanford University, 1966. No endorsement by SMSG is implied. By permission.

R. C. Scott and N. E. Sondak, *PL/I for Programmers.* Copyright © Addison-Wesley Publishing Company, 1970. By permission.

D. D. Spencer, *Programming with USA Standard Fortran and Fortran IV.* Copyright © 1969, Xerox Corporation. All rights reserved. By permission.

F. Stuart, *Fortran Programming.* Copyright © 1969 by Fredric Stuart. Reprinted by permission of John Wiley and Sons, Inc.

A. Vazsonyi, *Problem Solving by Digital Computers with PL/I Programming.* Copyright © Prentice-Hall, Inc., 1970. By permission.

T. M. Walker and W. W. Cotterman, *An Introduction to Computer Science and Algorithmic Processes.* Copyright © 1971 by Allyn and Bacon, Inc. Used by permission.

G. M. Weinberg, *PL/I Programming: A Manual of Style.* Copyright © McGraw-Hill, Inc., 1970. By permission.

CONTENTS

CONTENTS

PREFACE

Good programming cannot be taught by preaching generalities. The way to learn to program well is by seeing, over and over, how real programs can be improved by the application of a few principles of good practice and a little common sense. Practice in critical reading leads to skill in rewriting, which in turn leads to better writing.

This book is a study of a large number of "real" programs, each of which provides one or more lessons in style. We discuss the shortcomings of each example, rewrite it in a better way, then draw a general rule from the specific case. The approach is pragmatic and down-to-earth; we are more interested in improving current programming practice than in setting up an elaborate theory of how programming should be done. Consequently, this book can be used as a supplement in a programming course at any level, or as a refresher for experienced programmers.

The examples we give are all in Fortran and PL/I, since these languages are widely used and are sufficiently similar that a reading knowledge of one means that the other can also be *read* well enough. (We avoid complicated constructions in either language and explain unavoidable idioms as we encounter them.) *The principles of style, however, are applicable in all languages, including assembly codes.*

Our aim is to teach the elements of good style in a small space, so we concentrate on essentials. Rules are laid down throughout the text to emphasize the lessons learned. Each chapter ends with a summary and a set of "points to ponder," which provide exercises and a chance to investigate topics not fully covered in the text itself. Finally we collect our rules in one place for handy reference.

A word on the sources of the examples: *all* of the programs we use are taken from programming textbooks. Thus, we do not set up artificial programs to illustrate our points — we use finished products, written and published by experienced programmers. Since these examples are typically the first code seen by a novice programmer, we would hope that they would be models of good style. Unfortunately, we sometimes find that the opposite is true — textbook examples often demonstrate the state of the art of computer programming all too well. (We have done our best to play fair — we don't think that any of the programs are made to look bad by being quoted out of context.)

Let us state clearly, however, that we intend no criticism of textbook authors, either individually or as a class. Shortcomings show only that we are all human, and that under the pressure of a large, intellectually demanding task like writing a program or a book, it is much too easy to do some things imperfectly. We have no doubt that a few of our "good" programs will provide "bad" examples for some future writer — we hope only that he and his readers will learn from the experience of studying them carefully.

A manual of programming style could not have been written without the pioneering work of numerous people, many of whom have written excellent programming textbooks. D. D. McCracken and G. M. Weinberg, for instance, have long taught the virtues of simplicity and clarity. And the work of E. W. Dijkstra and Harlan Mills on structured programming has made possible our rules for properly specifying flow of control. The form and approach of this book has been strongly influenced by *The Elements of Style* by W. Strunk and E. B. White. We have tried to emulate their brevity by concentrating on the essential practical aspects of style.

We are indebted to many people for their help and encouragement. We would like especially to thank the authors and publishers who gave us permission to reproduce the computer programs used in this text. Their cooperation is greatly appreciated.

Our friends and colleagues at Bell Laboratories provided numerous useful suggestions, which we have incorporated, and saved us from more than one embarrassing blunder, which we have deleted. In particular, V. A. Vyssotsky bore with us through several revisions; for his perceptive comments and enthusiastic support at every stage of this book's evolution (and for several aphorisms we have shamelessly stolen) we are deeply grateful. We would also like to single out A. V. Aho, M. E. Lesk, M. D. McIlroy, and J. S. Thompson for the extensive time and assistance they gave to this project.

We were able to type the manuscript directly into a PDP 11/45, edit the source, check the programs, and set the final version in type — all with the help of a uniquely flexible operating system called UNIX. K. L. Thompson and D. M. Ritchie were the principal architects of UNIX; besides reading drafts, they helped us get the most out of the system while we were working on this book. J. F. Ossanna wrote the typesetting program and made several modifications for our special needs. We thank them.

Brian W. Kernighan

P. J. Plauger

I. INTRODUCTION

Consider the program fragment

```
    DO 14 I=1,N
    DO 14 J=1,N
 14 V(I,J)=(I/J)*(J/I)
```

A modest familiarity with Fortran tells us that this doubly nested DO loop assigns something to each element of an N by N matrix V. What are the values assigned? I and J are positive integer variables and, in Fortran, integer division truncates toward zero. Thus when I is less than J, (I/J) is zero; conversely, when J is less than I, (J/I) is zero. When I equals J, both factors are one. So (I/J)*(J/I) is one if and only if I equals J; otherwise it is zero. The program fragment puts ones on the diagonal of V and zeros everywhere else. (V becomes an identity matrix.) How clever!

Or is it?

Suppose you encountered this fragment in a larger program. If your knowledge of Fortran is sufficiently deep, you may have enjoyed the clever use of integer division. Possibly you were appalled that two divisions, a multiplication, and a conversion from integer to floating point were invoked when simpler mechanisms are available. More likely, you were driven to duplicating the reasoning we gave above to understand what is happening. Far more likely, you formed a vague notion that something useful is being put into an array and simply moved on. Only if motivated strongly, perhaps by the need to debug or to alter the program, would you be likely to go back and puzzle out the precise meaning.

A better version of the fragment is

```
C              MAKE V AN IDENTITY MATRIX
       DO 14 I = 1,N
          DO 12 J = 1,N
 12          V(I,J) = 0.0
 14       V(I,I) = 1.0
```

This zeros each row, then changes its diagonal element to one. The intent is now reasonably clear, and the code even happens to execute faster. Had we been programming in PL/I, we could have been more explicit:

1

```
          /* MAKE V AN IDENTITY MATRIX */
V = 0.0;
DO I = 1 TO N;
    V(I,I) = 1.0;
END;
```

In either case, it is more important to make the purpose of the code unmistakable than to display virtuosity. Even storage requirements and execution time are unimportant by comparison, for setting up an identity matrix must surely be but a small part of the whole program. The difficulty with obscure code is not that computers cannot understand it, but that it may not say what you thought it did.

Write clearly — don't be too clever.

Let's pause for a moment and look at what we've done. We studied part of a program, taken verbatim from a programming textbook, and discussed what was good about it and what was bad. Then we made it better. (Not necessarily perfect — just better.) And then we drew a rule or a general conclusion from our analysis and improvements, a rule that would have sounded like a sweeping generality in the abstract, but which makes sense and can be applied once you've seen a specific case.

The rest of the book will be much the same thing — an example from a text, discussion, improvements, and a rule, repeated over and over. When you have finished reading the book, you should be able to criticize your own code. More importantly, you should be able to write it better in the first place, with less need for criticism.

We have tried to sort the examples into a logical progression, but as we shall see, real programs are like prose — they often violate simultaneously a number of rules of good practice. Thus our classification scheme may sometimes seem arbitrary and we will often have to digress.

Most of the examples will be bigger than the one we just saw, but not excessively so; with the help of our discussion, you should be able to follow them even if you're a beginner. In fact, most of the bigger programs will shrink before your very eyes as we modify them. Sheer size is often an illusion, reflecting only a need for improvement.

The examples are all in either Fortran or PL/I, but if one or both of these languages is unfamiliar, that shouldn't intimidate you any more than size should. Although you may not be able to write a PL/I program, say, you will certainly be able to read one well enough to understand the point we are making, and the practice in reading will make learning PL/I that much easier.

For example, here is a small part of a PL/I program that we will discuss in more detail in Chapter 5:

```
        IF CTR > 45 THEN GO TO OVFLO;
        ELSE GO TO RDCARD;
OVFLO:
    ...
```

The first GOTO goes around the second GOTO, which seems a bit disorganized. If we rearrange, we get

```
        IF CTR <= 45 THEN GOTO RDCARD;
OVFLO:
    ...
```

One less statement, simpler logic, and, if we're lucky, we no longer need the label OVFLO. The lesson? Don't branch around branches: turn relational tests around if it makes the program easier to understand. We will soon see a Fortran example of exactly the same failing. This brings up an important point: although details vary from language to language, *the principles of style are the same*. Branching around branches is confusing in any language. So even if you program in Cobol or Basic or assembly language or whatever, the guidelines you find here still apply.

The reader might feel we're making a great fuss about a little thing in this last example. After all, it's still pretty obvious what the code says. The trouble is, although any single weakness causes no great harm, the cumulative effect of several confusing statements is code that is simply unintelligible.

Our next example is somewhat larger:

The following is a typical program to evaluate the square root (B) of a number (X):

```
   READ(5,1)X
 1 FORMAT(F10.5)
   A=X/2
 2 B=(X/A+A)/2
   C=B-A
   IF(C.LT.0)C=-C
   IF(C.LT.10.E-6)GOTO 3
   A=B
   GOTO 2
 3 WRITE(6,1)B
   STOP
   END
```

Because it is bigger, we can study it on several levels and learn something from each. For instance, before we analyze the code in detail, we might consider whether this program is truly "typical." It is unlikely that a square root routine would be a main program that reads its input from a file — a subroutine with an argument would be far more useful. Even assuming that we really do want a main program that computes square roots, is it likely that we would want it to compute only one before stopping?

This unfortunate tendency to write overly restricted code influences how we write programs that are supposed to be general. Soon enough we shall meet programs designed to keep track of exactly seventeen salesmen, to sort precisely 500 numbers, to trace through just one maze. We can only guess at how much of the program rewriting that goes on every day actually amounts to entering parameters via the compiler.

Let us continue with the square root program. It is an implementation of Newton's method, which is indeed at the heart of a typical library square root routine (although we need not go into precisely how it works). With proper data, the method converges rapidly. If X is negative, however, the program can go into an infinite loop. (Try it.) A good routine would instead provide an error return or a diagnostic message. And the program blows up in statement 2 if X is zero, a case that must be treated separately. The square root of zero should be reported as zero.

Even for strictly positive values of X this program can give garbage for an answer. The problem lies in the convergence test used:

```
C=B-A
IF(C.LT.0)C=-C
IF(C.LT.10.E-6)GOTO 3
```

To make effective use of the Fortran language, the line should read

```
C = ABS(C)
```

To avoid having someone misread 10.E−6 as "10 to the minus sixth power," the constant in the third line should read

```
1.0E-5
```

And to say what is meant without bombast, all three lines should be changed to

```
IF (ABS(B-A) .LT. 1.0E-5) GOTO 3
```

The test now reads clearly; it is merely wrong.

If X is large, it is quite possible that the absolute difference between successive trial roots will never be less than the arbitrary threshold of 1.0E−5 unless it is exactly zero, because of the finite precision with which computers represent numbers. It is a delicate question of numerical analysis whether this difference will always become zero. For small values of X, on the other hand, the criterion will be met long before a good approximation is attained. But if we replace the absolute convergence criterion by a test of whether the estimate is close enough *relative to the original data,* we should get five place accuracy for most positive arguments:

```
C                COMPUTE SQUARE ROOTS BY NEWTON'S METHOD
   10 READ(5,11) X
   11 FORMAT (F10.0)
      IF (X .GE. 0.0) GOTO 20
         WRITE(6,13) X
   13    FORMAT (' SQRT(', 1PE12.5, ') UNDEFINED')
         GOTO 10
   20 IF (X .GT. 0.0) GOTO 30
         B = 0.0
         GOTO 50
   30 B = 1.0
   40    A = B
         B = (X/A + A)/2.0
         IF (ABS((X/B)/B - 1.0) .GE. 1.0E-5) GOTO 40
   50 WRITE(6,51) X, B
   51 FORMAT(' SQRT(', 1PE12.5, ') = ', 1PE12.5)
         GOTO 10
         END
```

The modified program is still not a typical square root routine, nor do we wish to go into the detailed treatment of floating point arithmetic needed to make it one. The original example is, however, typical of programs in general: it profits from criticism and revision.

Let us conclude the chapter with another example that illustrates several failings. This program is a sorting routine.

```
      DIMENSION N(500)
      WRITE (6,6)
    6 FORMAT (1H1,26HNUMBERS IN ALGEBRAIC ORDER)
      DO 8 I=1,500
    8 READ (5,7) N(I)
    7 FORMAT (I4)
      DO 10 K=1,1999
      J=K-1000
      DO 10 I=1,500
      IF(N(I)-J)10,9,10
   10 CONTINUE
      STOP
    9 WRITE (6,95) N(I)
   95 FORMAT (1H ,I4)
      GO TO 10
      END
```

The code suffers not only from lack of generality, but from an ill-advised algorithm, some dubious coding practices, and even a typographical error. (The line

```
DO 10 I-1,500
```

is wrong: the "−" should be "=".) The program was contrived in part to illus-trate that the range of a DO loop can be extended by a transfer outside and back, even though in this case the inner DO loop *and* the code of the extended range can all be better written in line as

```
      DO 10 I = 1,500
          IF (N(I).EQ.J) WRITE(6,95) N(I)
 95       FORMAT(1X, I4)
 10 CONTINUE
```

More to the point is the question of whether programmers should be en-couraged to use extended ranges in the first place. Jumping around unneces-sarily in a computer program has proved to be a fruitful source of errors, and usually indicates that the programmer is not entirely in control of his code. The apparently random statement numbers we see in this example are often a symptom of the same disorder.

The program has other flaws. It reads in 500 numbers, one per card, and sorts them about as inefficiently as possible — by comparing each number with all integers between −999 and +999. It does this once, for only one set of numbers, then stops.

But wait. With an I4 input format, it is possible to read positive numbers as large as 9999, since we can leave out the plus sign; the program as it stands will fail to list four-digit numbers. To correct the oversight will slow the algo-rithm by a factor of more than five, without extending its generality in the least. Extending this method to handle larger integers would slow it by orders of mag-nitude, and to ask it to handle floating point numbers would be unthinkable.

We will not attempt to rewrite this code, since we disagree with its basic approach. (Chapter 6 contains several better sorting programs.) We just want to show that the same program can be viewed from different perspectives, and that the job of critical reading doesn't end when you find a typo or even a poor coding practice. In the chapters to come we will explore the issues touched on here and several others that strongly affect programming style.

We begin, in Chapter 2, with a study of how to express statements clearly. Writing arithmetic expressions and conditional (IF) statements is usually the first aspect of computer programming that is taught. It is important to master these fundamentals before becoming too involved with other language features.

Chapter 3 treats the structure of computer programs. Structure is mostly concerned with how flow of control is specified through the executable state-ments, but it also touches on how to represent data to assist processing.

Chapter 4 examines input and output: how to render programs less vulner-able to bad input data and what to output to obtain maximum benefit from a run. A number of common blunders are studied in Chapter 5, and tips are given on how to spot such errors and correct them.

Contrary to popular practice, efficiency and documentation are reserved for the last two chapters, 6 and 7. While both of these topics are important and warrant study, we feel they have received proportionately too much attention — particularly in introductory courses — at the expense of clarity and general good style.

A few words on the ground rules we have used in criticizing programs:

(1) Programs are presented in a form as close to the original as our typescript permits. Formatting, typographical errors, and syntax errors are as in the original. (Exception: two PL/I programs have been translated from the 48-character set into the 60-character set.)

(2) We regularly abstract parts of programs to focus better on the essential points. We believe that the failings we discuss are inherent in the code shown, and not caused or aggravated by abstracting. We have tried not to quote out of context. We have tried throughout to solve essentially the same problem as the original version did, so comparisons may be made fairly.

(3) We will not fault an example for using non-standard language features (for example, mixed mode arithmetic in Fortran) unless the use is quite unusual or dangerous. Most compilers accept non-standard constructions, and standards themselves change with time. Remember, though, that unusual features are rarely portable, and are the least resistant to changes in their environment.

Our own Fortran hews closely to the current American National Standards Institute (ANSI) version, except for our use of quoted Hollerith strings (we refuse to count characters). PL/I programs meet the standard set by IBM's checkout compiler, version 1.2.

(4) In our discussions of numerical algorithms (like the square root routine above) we will not try to treat all possible pathological cases; the defenses needed against overflow, significance loss, and other numerical pitfalls are beyond the scope of this book. But we do insist that at least the rudimentary precautions (like using relative tests instead of absolute, and avoiding division by zero) be taken to ensure good results for reasonable inputs.

(5) Every line of code in this book has been compiled, directly from the text, which is in machine-readable form. All of our programs have been tested (Fortran on a Honeywell 6070, PL/I on an IBM 370/165). Our Fortran programs have also been run through a verifier to monitor compliance with the ANSI standard.

Nevertheless, mistakes can occur. We encourage you to view

with suspicion anything we say that looks peculiar. Test it, try it
out. Don't treat computer printout as gospel. If you learn to be
wary of everyone else's programs, you will be better able to
check your own.

POINTS TO PONDER

1.1 A matrix with N rows and N columns has N^2 elements. So to initialize such a matrix requires N^2 assignments. To multiply two N by N matrices together, or to invert an N by N matrix, involves on the order of N^3 operations by classical methods. (These are the sorts of things that matrix manipulation programs do.) Give arguments to support the following conjectures:

   If $N \geq 10$, the time required to initialize a matrix is not very important.

   If $N < 10$, the time required to initialize a matrix is not very important. (Hint: input and output conversions are time consuming compared to arithmetic.)

1.2 In the square root routine, we saw that testing for convergence against an absolute threshold like 1.0E−5 is perilous. We recommended testing instead against some sort of relative standard. How can the arithmetic statement function

```
RELDIF(X,Y) = ABS(X-Y)/AMAX1(ABS(X),ABS(Y))
```

be used in the example? (AMAX1 is the Fortran function that returns the maximum of two or more floating point numbers as floating point.)

This function is relatively well-behaved for values that might be encountered in the square-root routine. In more general applications, are there any values of X and Y that might cause trouble?

II. EXPRESSION

Writing a computer program eventually boils down to writing a sequence of statements in the language at hand. How each of those statements is expressed determines in large measure the intelligibility of the whole; no amount of commenting, formatting, or supplementary documentation can entirely replace well expressed statements. After all, they determine what the program actually *does*.

It is easy to mistake a sequence of overly-simple expressions for profundity. An extreme example of this is

```
IF A>B THEN DO;
LARGE=A;
GO TO CHECK;
END;
LARGE=B;
CHECK: IF LARGE>C THEN GO TO OUTPUT;
LARGE=C;
OUTPUT: ...
```

Seven and a half lines of code and two labels are used; surely *something* is happening. After a bit of study we see that, by the end of the code sequence, LARGE is set to the largest of A, B, and C.

There are a number of ways to do this computation. If our purpose is to teach how to compute the maximum, we write

```
LARGE = A;
IF B>LARGE THEN LARGE = B;
IF C>LARGE THEN LARGE = C;
```

which is direct and to the point. Labels and GOTOs are not needed.

Say what you mean, simply and directly.

But if we are just trying to get the job done, rather than making a point about relational operators, we write

11

```
      LARGE = MAX(A,B,C);
```

in the first place. Library functions let you build on the work of others, instead of starting from scratch each time.

Use library functions.

   Peculiar modes of expression often arise out of attempts to write "efficient" code. The programmer has some knowledge about how his compiler generates code, so he uses only those expressions that he "knows" are "better." For instance

```
   10 F1=X1-X2*X2
      F2=1.0-X2
      FX=F1*F1+F2*F2
C NOTE THAT IT IS MORE EFFICIENT TO COMPUTE
C F1*F1 THAN TO COMPUTE F1**2.
```

   Whether "efficient" means "takes less time" or "takes less machine code," the comment is not always true. Many compilers recognize the special case F1**2 and generate the same code as for F1*F1. Some compilers would, in fact, generate shorter and faster code for

```
   10 FX = (X1 - X2**2)**2 + (1.0 - X2)**2
```

than for the original version. (Ours produced 15 instructions for the original version, 13 for the revision.) This rendition also happens to be more readable and eliminates the temporary variables F1 and F2. The fewer temporary variables in a program, the less chance there is that one will not be properly initialized, or that one will be altered unexpectedly before it is used, and the easier the program is to understand.

Avoid temporary variables.

   Even if the comment about efficiency were true in a particular environment, there is still little justification for using the more obscure mode of expression. We shall discuss the question of efficiency further in Chapter 6. For now, we observe simply that a program usually has to be read several times in the process of getting it debugged. The harder it is for *people* to grasp the intent of any given section, the longer it will be before the program becomes operational. Trying to outsmart a compiler defeats much of the purpose of using one.

Write clearly — don't sacrifice
clarity for "efficiency."

A variation of this is

```
/*    NOTE THAT '110010' IN BINARY IS '50' IN DECIMAL     */
/*         THIS WILL BE USED FOR LINE COUNTING            */
    ...
       IF NO>101111B THEN DO ; PUT PAGE; NO=0B;
                         END;
```

The programmer evidently hopes to avoid a run-time type-conversion by using FIXED BINARY constants in expressions involving FIXED BINARY variables. The comment underlines the fact that human beings are not likely to know the binary representation of 50. Yet we are expected to recognize a binary 47 on the basis of this one hint. One of the first services to be automated in early computer languages was the conversion of decimal to binary. It would be a shame if we were forced to think in binary, after all these years, by misinformed considerations of "efficiency." (Most compilers will convert "47" to binary at compile time, by the way. Those that will not must certainly provide worse inefficiencies to worry about.)

Let the machine do the dirty work.

Repeated patterns of code catch the eye when scanning listings. Since the computer is a tool for handling repetitious operations, we should be alerted by such patterns to look for oversights — why didn't the programmer let the computer do his repeating for him? In the middle of a program for manipulating triangles we see the fragment

```
C     COMPUTE LENGTHS OF SIDES
      AB = SQRT((X2 - X1)**2 + (Y2 - Y1)**2)
      AC = SQRT((X3 - X1)**2 + (Y3 - Y1)**2)
      BC = SQRT((X3 - X2)**2 + (Y3 - Y2)**2)
C     COMPUTE AREA
      S = (AB + BC + AC) / 2.0
      AREA = SQRT(S * (S-BC) * (S-AC) * (S-AB)
      ...
C     COMPUTE ANGLES
      ALPHA = ATANF((4.0*AREA) / (AC**2 + AB**2 - BC**2))
      BETA = ATANF((4.0*AREA) / (AB**2 + BC**2 - AC**2))
      GAMMA = ATANF((4.0*AREA) / (AC**2 + BC**2 - AB**2))
```

We can see immediately the advantage of defining two arithmetic statement functions:

```
SIDE(XA,YA,XB,YB) = SQRT((XA-XB)**2 + (YA-YB)**2)
ANGLE(SAREA,SA,SB,SC) = ATAN2(4.0*SAREA,
$                               SA**2 + SB**2 - SC**2)
```

so that we can write

```
AB = SIDE(X1,Y1,X2,Y2)
AC = SIDE(X1,Y1,X3,Y3)
BC = SIDE(X2,Y2,X3,Y3)
...
ALPHA = ANGLE(AREA,AC,AB,BC)
BETA = ANGLE(AREA,AB,BC,AC)
GAMMA = ANGLE(AREA,AC,BC,AB)
```

(We have used "$" as the continuation character, because it is the only standard Fortran character without any other syntactic meaning. It minimizes the chance for confusion.)

This is not only easier to write but also easier to modify. For instance the Fortran II name ATANF should be changed whenever possible to the Fortran IV standard ATAN. In fact, the form

```
ATAN(Y/X)
```

should always be changed to

```
ATAN2(Y,X)
```

which correctly handles right-angled triangles instead of causing a division by zero when Y/X is evaluated. Only one change was needed in the function definition to correct all three calculations; we were more likely to get it right. (The program also contains a typographical error:

```
AREA = SQRT(S * (S-BC) * (S-AC) * (S-AB)
```

needs a balancing right parenthesis on the end.)

Fortran's arithmetic statement function is unfortunately restricted to one-line expressions, and is thus of limited usefulness. When the operation to be done is more complex, write a regular subroutine or function. The ease of later

comprehending, debugging, and changing the program will compensate for any
overhead caused by adding the extra modules.

---

*Replace repetitive expressions by calls
to a common function.*

Another eye-catching repeat appears in

```
      R = 12.
      AL = 24.
      TIME = 0.
      THETA = 0.
      DELTH = 2. * 3.1416 / 100.
      DO 18 I = 1,100
      X = R*(1. - COS(THETA)) + L - L*SQRT(1. - (R*SIN(THETA)/L)**2)
      THETA = THETA + DELTH
      XNEW= R * (1. - COS(THETA)) + L - L*SQRT(1. - (R*SIN(THETA)/L)**2)
      VEL = (XNEW - X) / 0.01
      TIME = TIME + 0.01
   18 WRITE (2,8) TIME, THETA, XNEW, VEL
    8 FORMAT (4F9.2)
      STOP
      END
```

Our first impulse is to define another arithmetic statement function for the gan-
gling expression that appears twice, but closer inspection shows a more fundamental oversight.

The program computes X and its first derivative VEL at each of 100 successive points. Two adjacent values of X must be known to find VEL, so the program dutifully computes both on each iteration, even though one value is already known from the previous iteration. The elaborate expression is computed
twice as often as necessary.

There is also an error: L is used in both expressions where AL is certainly
intended. Less serious, but potentially troublesome, is the practice of incre-
menting a floating point variable many times (see Chapter 5). To keep arithmetic errors from piling up and to make the code clearer, we are better off computing TIME and THETA from I on each iteration. Putting everything together
gives:

```
      REAL L
      R = 12.0
      L = 24.0
      X = 0.0
      DO 20 I = 1,100
         TIME = FLOAT(I)/100.0
         THETA = 2.0 * 3.141593 * TIME
         XNEW = R*(1.0 - COS(THETA)) + L -
     $          L*SQRT(1.0 - (R*SIN(THETA)/L)**2)
         VEL = (XNEW - X)/0.01
         WRITE(2,10) TIME, THETA, XNEW, VEL
   10    FORMAT(4F9.2)
         X = XNEW
   20 CONTINUE
      STOP
      END
```

Since we have saved a hundred function evaluations, we will not worry about computing 2π inside the loop. We also decided to stick with the identifier L, instead of changing all occurrences to AL. The original problem was stated in terms of R and L; it is usually safer to remain consistent with this notation than to try to remember the translation all the time. This is one of those unfortunate occasions when standard Fortran notation is at odds with the usage desired. You can argue it either way, but we decided in this case that adding the statement

```
      REAL L
```

is better than renaming the variable.

Arithmetic expressions in Fortran and PL/I also differ sometimes from the way we intuitively tend to write them. We are accustomed, in writing algebra, to bind multiplication tighter than division. That is, we assume that if we write

```
      A*B/2.0*C
```

it means

```
      (A*B)/(2.0*C)   /* WRONG */
```

But in Fortran or PL/I the interpretation is

```
      ((A*B)/2.0)*C
```

Only by using parentheses or rearranging the computation can we avoid potential confusion.

A more insidious operator ambiguity occurs in this expression from an arctangent routine:

```
TERM = TERM*(-X**2)/DENOM
```

Is X negated and then squared, or is it squared and then negated? Fortran reference manuals seldom treat such fine points in detail; this may be a hard question to answer without running a test program. As a matter of fact the ANSI standard for Fortran calls for the latter interpretation (fortunate in this case) — the variable X is squared and then negated — but the line should still be rewritten as:

```
TERM = -TERM*(X**2)/DENOM
```

The first form invites misunderstanding on the part of the reader, if not the compiler.

Parenthesize to avoid ambiguity.

Variable names can also be either safe or dangerous:

```
8 NO5S = NO5S + 1
```

Now was that "N, letter O, five, S," or "N, zero, five, S," or even "NOSS"? The possibilities for error are numerous. Would you trust someone else to type corrections for this program? Mixtures of similar characters (letter O and digit 0, letter I and digit 1, etc.) are unsafe, as are long identifiers that differ only at the end. Use XPOS and YPOS, not POSITIONX and POSITIONY.

Similar identifiers are dangerous in general. One program contains the improbable sequence

```
N = K
N = K**2
NNN = K**3
```

It is only when, much further down, we read

```
WRITE(6,60)N,NN,NNN, ...
```

that the typographical error in the second line becomes clear. A better choice of names here is N, NSQ, NCUBE. Try to choose names that differ widely; typos and misspellings are less likely to be disguised.

Choose variable names that won't be confused.

We have discussed arithmetic expressions quite a bit, but conditional expressions are at least as important in writing programs. In either PL/I or Fortran, conditional expressions nearly always involve at least one IF statement, which controls whether or not another statement is executed, on the basis of some condition. PL/I allows the controlled statement to be compound, and therefore arbitrarily complex, but we will save complicated examples for Chapter 3. Most of the remaining examples here will be in Fortran, since that language encourages greater atrocities in the form of conditional expressions.

Part of the reason for this is historical. Fortran II had only the arithmetic IF statement, which does not perform as we suggested in the previous paragraph. Instead it causes a branch to one of three statement numbers, depending on whether an arithmetic expression is negative, zero, or positive. The logical IF was added to Fortran IV as a cleaner way of expressing conditionals. It should almost always be used instead of the arithmetic IF, especially when two of the three labels are the same.

The arithmetic IF is next to unreadable, as this subroutine from a sort program shows:

```
C     MERGES LISTS P AND Q ONTO LISTS R AND S
 1 SUBROUTINE MERGE(P,Q,R,S,N)
 2 DIMENSION P(N),Q(N),R(N),S(N)
 3 LP=1
 4 LQ=1
 5 LR=1
 6 LS=1
 7 CALL ORDER(P,Q,R,LP,LQ,LR,N)
 8 IF(P(LP))10, 9,10
 9 IF(Q(LQ))10,13,10
10 CALL ORDER(P,Q,S,LP,LQ,LS,N)
11 IF(P(LP)) 7,12, 7
12 IF(Q(LQ)) 7,13, 7
13 RETURN
   END
```

The presence of all those superfluous statement numbers doesn't help matters; we cannot tell, without scanning the whole program, what statements can be reached via some branch. And what if a line should be added or deleted? Unused statement numbers should be disposed of promptly. But even without them, we are reduced to drawing lines all over the listing to trace the flow when arithmetic IFs are used.

See how much more readable we can make the code from statement 7 onward:

```
7 CALL ORDER(P,Q,R,LP,LQ,LR,N)
  IF (P(LP) .EQ. 0.0 .AND. Q(LQ) .EQ. 0.0) RETURN
  CALL ORDER(P,Q,S,LP,LQ,LS,N)
  IF (P(LP) .EQ. 0.0 .AND. Q(LQ) .EQ. 0.0) RETURN
  GOTO 7
  END
```

(Testing whether one floating point variable is exactly equal to another is usually risky, as we shall see in Chapter 5; it is safe here only because "0.0" is a flag, not a computed value.)

Occasionally the third branch of an arithmetic IF can serve to direct an "impossible" condition to error-handling code. Even when all three branches of the arithmetic IF are distinct, however, readability is often better served by substituting two logical IFs and a GOTO.

Avoid the Fortran arithmetic IF.

A conditional expression can also be disguised by using a computed GOTO:

```
   GOTO(65,70),PRNT
65 WRITE(6,105) X
70 ...
```

The computed GOTO has a definite place, but this is not it. Since labels 65 and 70 appear nowhere else in the program, this code is certainly better written as

```
IF (PRNT.NE.2) WRITE(6,105) X
```

to eliminate the two statement numbers. Now we can tell at á glance that there is only one way to reach the WRITE statement.

The influence of the arithmetic IF often extends into misuse of the logical IF. Two examples are

```
IF((X(I) — X(N)) .LE. 0.) GO TO 300
```

which should be written

```
IF (X(I) .LE. X(N)) GOTO 300
```

and

```
        IF (MOD(K,N1).NE.0) GO TO 9
        WRITE (6,4) K,X
      9 ...
```

which is better rendered as

```
        IF (MOD(K,N1).EQ.0) WRITE(6,4) K, X
```

The first is a literal translation of an arithmetic into a logical IF. The second shows a tendency to make all IFs into control branches, even when they do not have to be. Such usage eventually leads to circumlocutions like

```
        GRVAL = A(1)
        DO 25 I = 2,10
        IF (A(I).GT.GRVAL) GO TO 30
        GO TO 25
     30 GRVAL = A(I)
     25 CONTINUE
```

The IF controls a branch that branches around the branch that branches around the statement we wanted to do in the first place. Turning things right side up gives

```
        GRVAL = A(1)
        DO 25 I = 2,10
           IF (A(I).GT.GRVAL) GRVAL = A(I)
     25 CONTINUE
```

We leave it to the reader to decide whether the IF statement should be replaced by

```
        GRVAL = AMAX1(GRVAL, A(I))
```

when we are finding the larger of just two elements.

Avoid unnecessary branches.

A failure to state clearly the underlying logic can lead to tangled control flow, as in this program for a rudimentary computer dating service:

```
      LOGICAL FEM(8),MALE(8)
      READ(5,6)IGIRL,(FEM(I),I=1,8)
    9 READ(5,6)IBOY,(MALE(I),I=1,8)
      DO 8I= 1,8
      IF(FEM(I)) GO TO 7
      IF(.NOT.MALE(I)) GO TO 8
      GO TO 9
    7 IF(.NOT.MALE(I)) GO TO 9
    8 CONTINUE
      WRITE(2,10) IBOY
    6 FORMAT (I5,8L1)
   10 FORMAT (10X,I5)
      GO TO 9
      STOP
      END
```

We have to look long and hard at this jungle of IFs and GOTOs before the light dawns. The program is supposed to write IBOY only if each of the MALE(I) has the same truth value as the corresponding FEM(I). Standard Fortran does not allow us to ask directly if two LOGICAL variables are equal or not, but we can still improve readability by using .AND. and .OR.:

```
      LOGICAL FEM(8), MALE(8)
      READ(5,10) IGIRL, FEM
   10 FORMAT (I5, 8L1)
   20 READ(5,10) IBOY, MALE
      DO 30 I = 1,8
         IF( (FEM(I) .AND. .NOT.MALE(I)) .OR.
    $        (MALE(I) .AND. .NOT.FEM(I)) ) GOTO 20
   30 CONTINUE
      WRITE(2,40) IBOY
   40 FORMAT (10X, I5)
      GOTO 20
      END
```

This tells us directly that the program will go on to read the next input line, without printing IBOY, if any of the FEM(I) differ from its corresponding MALE(I). We also deleted the inaccessible STOP statement and the explicit indexing in the READ statements, and numbered the statements systematically.

Don't use conditional branches
as a substitute for a logical expression.

As an aside, the dating program provides a simple example of how an appropriate data structure can make programming easier. With INTEGER variables instead of LOGICAL, we can make the desired comparison directly:

```
    INTEGER FEM(8), MALE(8)
    READ(5,10) IGIRL, FEM
 10 FORMAT(I5, 8I1)
 20 READ(5,10) IBOY, MALE
    DO 30 I = 1,8
        IF( FEM(I) .NE. MALE(I) ) GOTO 20
 30 CONTINUE
    ...
```

The data will also have to be changed, from Ts and Fs to ones and zeros, but this is a simple mechanical operation.

The expression in parentheses in a logical IF statement is of type LOGICAL; its value is either .TRUE. or .FALSE.. Most of the time we use just a relational operator, such as .LE. or .EQ., to determine the truth value of the condition. But we can, if we wish, use the Boolean operators .AND., .OR., and .NOT. to make arbitrarily complex logical expressions. Boolean algebra is not used nearly as widely as ordinary arithmetic, so we must write logical expressions more carefully lest we confuse the reader.

Consider the sequence

```
 6 IF(X1.GE.ARRAY(I)) GO TO 2
   IF(ARRAY(I).LT.X2) ICOUNT=ICOUNT+1
 2 ...
```

It takes a while to realize that ICOUNT is incremented only if ARRAY(I) lies between X1 and X2. Inversions slow down reading comprehension and should be avoided. Rewriting gives:

```
 6 IF (X1.LT.ARRAY(I) .AND. ARRAY(I).LT.X2) ICOUNT = ICOUNT+1
```

It is much easier to tell at a glance what the logic implies.

It is simpler to write good logical expressions in PL/I, but that is no guarantee that all expressions will be written as clearly as they can be:

```
 IF K=0 | (¬(PRINT='YES' | PRINT='NO')) THEN DO;
```

The inversion and double parentheses slow comprehension. It seems better to distribute the "not" operation through the parenthesized expression. De Morgan's rules

```
    ¬(A | B) <=> ¬A & ¬B
    ¬(A & B) <=> ¬A | ¬B
```

tell us how:

```
IF K=0 | (PRINT¬='YES' & PRINT¬='NO') THEN DO;
```

The expression is still not simple, but it is now in a form that more closely resembles how we speak. Note that we elected to keep one set of parentheses, to make the operator binding unambiguous.

If a logical expression is hard to understand,
try transforming it.

Using De Morgan's rules often improves the readability of programs by simplifying logical expressions. But care should be exercised in how they are applied, for several inversions must be made. An example of the pitfalls of inverting logic comes from this routine to access a sparse matrix stored as a linear table. The function is supposed to return a table value if it finds a matching row *and* column; otherwise it returns zero.

```
      FUNCTION SPARSE(I,J)
      COMMON /SP/ N,NROW(500),NCOL(500),VALUE(500)
      DO 10 K = 1,N
      IF (NROW(K).NE.I .AND. NCOL(K).NE.J) GO TO 10
      SPARSE = VALUE(K)
      GO TO 999
   10 CONTINUE
      SPARSE = 0.0
  999 RETURN
      END
```

By definition the sparse array has a value stored at VALUE(K) for (I,J) if

```
NROW(K).EQ.I .AND. NCOL(K).EQ.J
```

Negating this for the IF statement gives

```
.NOT.(NROW(K).EQ.I) .OR. .NOT.(NCOL(K).EQ.J)
```

or

```
NROW(K).NE.I .OR. NCOL(K).NE.J
```

Compare this line with the IF statement in the function. FUNCTION SPARSE is wrong; it will return the first value where *either* I or J is matched. The .AND. must be changed to .OR.. (This error has been corrected in later printings of the text from which it was taken.) Actually, the code would be more direct if it were written with the test stated positively:

```
      FUNCTION SPARSE(I, J)
      COMMON /SP/ N, NROW(500), NCOL(500), VALUE(500)
      DO 10 K = 1,N
         IF (NROW(K).EQ.I .AND. NCOL(K).EQ.J) GOTO 20
   10 CONTINUE
      SPARSE = 0.0
      RETURN
C
   20 SPARSE = VALUE(K)
      RETURN
      END
```

We have discussed a number of small examples where expressions were either hard to read, misleading, or downright incorrect. Let us conclude this chapter with one larger example, to show how quickly a program can get out of hand when you fail to look after the little things. (This is the first big PL/I program we have looked at — don't let it frighten you.) The program finds the area under the parabola $Y=X^2$, between $X=0$ and $X=1$, using a trapezoidal rule and several different step sizes.

```
TRAPZ: PROCEDURE OPTIONS (MAIN);
    DECLARE MSSG1 CHARACTER (20);
      MSSG1 = 'AREA UNDER THE CURVE';
    DECLARE MSSG2 CHARACTER (23);
      MSSG2 = 'BY THE TRAPAZOIDAL RULE';
    DECLARE MSSG3 CHARACTER (16);
      MSSG3 = 'FOR DELTA X = 1/';
    DECLARE I FIXED DECIMAL (2);
    DECLARE J FIXED DECIMAL (2);
    DECLARE L FIXED DECIMAL (7,6);
    DECLARE M FIXED DECIMAL (7,6);
    DECLARE N FIXED DECIMAL (2);
    DECLARE AREA1 FIXED DECIMAL (8,6);
    DECLARE AREA FIXED DECIMAL  (8,6);
    DECLARE LMTS FIXED DECIMAL (5,4);
        PUT SKIP EDIT (MSSG1)  (X(9), A(20));
        PUT SKIP EDIT (MSSG2)  (X(7), A(23));
        PUT SKIP EDIT (' ') (A(1));
    AREA = 0;
        DO K = 4 TO 10;
            M = 1 / K;
            N = K - 1;
        LMTS = .5 * M;
```

continued on next page

```
            I = 1;
          DO J = 1 TO N;
            L = (I / K) ** 2;
    AREA1 = .5 * M * (2 * L);
    AREA = AREA + AREA1;
       IF I = N THEN CALL OUT;
        ELSE I = I + 1;
      END;
    END;
 OUT: PROCEDURE;
        AREA = AREA + LMTS;
    PUT SKIP EDIT  (MSSG3,K,AREA) (X(2),A(16),F(2),X(6),
          F(9,6));
      AREA = 0;
    RETURN;
    END;
  END;
```

Held at arm's length, this program looks pretty impressive. There is a large assortment of data declarations, followed by a computation that is evidently complex enough to warrant a sub-procedure. Declarations are neatly aligned, and the executable statements are staggered so as to indicate several levels of control nesting. There are text strings to suggest the intent of the program, and mnemonic identifiers to give hints about how the results are obtained. The general impression conveyed is that this is a moderately complicated problem that has been carefully coded and is now well under control.

Closer inspection, however, shows quite the opposite.

Each output message is used only once, and would be better placed in the PUT statement that uses it instead of being separately declared and initialized by an assignment. (One message is even misspelled.) The first two PUT statements can be combined into

```
PUT SKIP EDIT ('AREA UNDER THE CURVE',
               'BY THE TRAPEZOIDAL RULE')
               (X(9), A, SKIP, X(7), A);
```

and the bizarre

```
PUT SKIP EDIT(' ') (A(1));
```

changed into a simple PUT SKIP. And there is no reason to specify character-string lengths in the A format items; computers count much better than people do.

The purpose of the assignment

```
M = 1 / K;
```

is unclear. Does it defend against some mysterious conversion? Is it to convey geometrical insight? Or does the programmer worry that computers divide more slowly than they multiply? It is a rare program that can be speeded up significantly by changing divisions into multiplications, and this is not one of them — M appears only twice. Efficiency cannot be of grave importance anyway, not when the code contains the statement

```
AREA1 = .5 * M * (2 * L);
```

which has two superfluous multiplications (but no divisions). M can be eliminated. Similarly, N, LMTS, L and AREA1 vanish as the obvious substitutions are made.

We can now remove all those declarations with the strange precisions needed for intermediate results. The remaining declarations consist of just two different types. A close look reveals that K is not declared, even though all other arithmetic variables are. By default K will be FIXED BINARY, so a number of type conversions will occur, to no advantage. K should be included in the declarations.

With all the extraneous assignments removed, it is easier to see the underlying structure. It is also easy to see that the indentations reflect little of what is going on. But what is the purpose of the variable I? It is laboriously kept equal to J so that OUT can be called at the end of the last iteration. Clearly I is not needed, for J could be used for the test. But the test is not needed; OUT could be called just after the inner DO loop has terminated. But OUT need not be called at all, for its code could just as well appear in the one place it is invoked. The structure simplifies remarkably.

Now we can see that the summing variable AREA is supposed to be initialized at the beginning of each loop on K. This is much better practice than clearing it before entering the loop and again at the end of each iteration — in a remote procedure at that. Our major criticism of the procedure OUT is not its existence, since it was there for pedagogical reasons, but that it changes AREA and uses LMTS when it does not have to. Destroying modularity in this fashion, referring to seemingly local variables in unexpected places, is an invitation to future bugs. When code is rearranged, or the use of such non-local variables is changed, errors are almost certain to be introduced.

Putting all our improvements together gives:

```
TRAPZ: PROCEDURE OPTIONS(MAIN);
    DECLARE (J,K) FIXED DECIMAL (2),
        AREA  FIXED DECIMAL (8,6);

    PUT SKIP EDIT ('AREA UNDER THE CURVE',
                    'BY THE TRAPEZOIDAL RULE')
                    (X(9), A, SKIP, X(7), A);
    PUT SKIP;
```

continued on next page

```
DO K = 4 TO 10;
   AREA = 0.5/K;

   DO J = 1 TO K-1;
      AREA = AREA + ((J/K)**2)/K;
   END;

   PUT SKIP EDIT ('FOR DELTA X=1/', K, AREA)
                 (X(2), A, F(2), X(6), F(9,6));
   END;
END TRAPZ;
```

The program now reflects how straightforward the calculation really is. (Both the original and our version are quite specific to this one problem. See problem 2.3.)

The original program gave correct answers, yet we were able to improve upon it considerably. It is clear that successful operation is no guarantee of a good program. The changes we made were not designed to decrease execution time (which was unchanged) or to decrease storage utilization (which improved by thirty percent). Had we been concerned with optimization in the usual sense, we would have factored $1/K^3$ out of the AREA calculation.

What then did we improve? Readability, principally, but also locality and simplicity of structure. AREA is initialized just before it is used, not in two widely separated and illogical places. The calculation now proceeds from top to bottom without the excursion to a sub-procedure. The original program was puffed up with needless declarations and expressions, with over-simple computations and over-complex control structure. Programs are not used once and discarded, nor are they run forever without change. They evolve. The new version of the integration program has a greater likelihood of surviving changes later without acquiring bugs. It assists instead of intimidating those who must maintain it. This will be the goal of all our revisions.

To summarize some of the specific points of this chapter:

(1) Write clearly. If you find your code branching around branches or around single statements, turn relational tests around. For each GOTO, ask if it could be cleanly eliminated. Avoid constructions like Fortran's arithmetic IF that force GOTOs and labels upon you.

(2) Be sparing with temporary variables. The clutter from too many temporaries confuses readers (including you), and may well thwart an optimizing compiler.

(3) Add parentheses and alter too-similar identifiers to avoid any possibility of misunderstanding. Be unambiguous.

(4) Don't build *all* of your own tools: use standard library functions like MAX and ABS. If no function exists, write your own as a separate function, and add it to your private library.

POINTS TO PONDER

2.1 How long do you think it would take you to make this Fortran expression for the root of a quadratic syntactically and semantically correct?

```
ROOT1 = (-B + SQRT(B**2 - 4AC)/2A
```

Six characters *have* to be added, counting decimal points after floating point literals. Did you use eight on your first try? Which version is easier to read? Do you think knowing the quadratic formula by heart helps or hinders proofreading?

2.2 In the trapezoidal integration program discussed above, suppose you had been assigned the job of writing procedure OUT, while someone else wrote the main procedure. How many things do the two of you have to agree on — names of variables, who initializes what — before you can write OUT as it stands? If each initialized his own variables, and the values to be printed were passed as parameters as in

```
CALL OUT (K, AREA);
```

how many things do you then have to agree on?

2.3 Consider the effort needed to change both versions of the trapezoidal integration program to deal with an arbitrary function F(X) between arbitrary limits A and B. Which conversion represents an easier task and why?

2.4 The following program counts sentences, words and characters in a text. A slash marks the end of the text. Rewrite it using logical IFs instead of arithmetic IFs. How many labels are now necessary?

```
      INTEGER C,KT,BUFR(72),BLANK,COMMA,SCOL,DASH,SLSH,PEROD,NW,NC,NS
      REAL AWS,ASW
      DATA BLANK,COMMA,SCOL,DASH,SLSH,PEROD/' ',',',';',','-','/',','.'/,
     * NW,NC,NS,KT,C/0,0,0,73,' '/
101 FORMAT(1H1,35X,'INPUT TEXT')
102 FORMAT(72A1)
103 FORMAT(4X,72A1)
104 FORMAT(///,26X,'NUMBER OF SENTENCES=',I8,/,19X,'AVERAGE NUMBER OF
     *WORDS/SENTENCE=',F8.2,/20X,'AVERAGE NUMBER OF SYMBOLS/WORD=',F8.2)
      WRITE(6,101)
 10 READ(5,102) BUFR
      WRITE(6,103) BUFR
      KT=KT-72
      IF(C-PEROD) 20,35,20
 20 C=BUFR(KT)
 25 IF(C-PEROD) 40,30,40
```

continued on next page

```
30 NS=NS+1
   NW=NW+1
   KT=KT+3
   IF(KT-72) 35,35,10
35 C=BUFR(KT)
   IF(C-SLSH) 25,75,25
40 IF(C-BLANK) 50,45,50
45 NW=NW+1
   GO TO 70
50 IF(C-COMMA) 55,70,55
55 IF(C-SCOL) 60,70,60
60 IF(C-DASH) 65,70,65
65 NC=NC+1
70 KT=KT+1
   IF(KT-72) 20,20,10
75 AWS=FLOAT(NW)/NS
   ASW=FLOAT(NC)/NW
   WRITE(6,104) NS,AWS,ASW
   CALL EXIT
   END
```

2.5 In the preceding program, what happens if a period occurs in column 71 or
72 of an input card? What happens if more than one blank separates two
words? What happens if there are leading or trailing blanks on a line?
What happens if a sentence ends with a question mark? What else
happens? Rewrite the program to make it less vulnerable.

III. STRUCTURE

A computer program is organized naturally around its data representation and the statements that determine its flow of control. These define the *structure* of a program. There is no sharp distinction between expression and organization; it is more a question of scope. In the previous chapter we were concerned with the details of expressing each statement well. Here we will concentrate on matters of style that affect the program as a whole.

A program frequently turns out ill-formed because its data representation is inappropriate for the job at hand. We have already seen one example of this: the simple change from LOGICAL variables to INTEGERs clarified the dating service program of Chapter 2.

Here is another example where data structure makes all the difference. It is from a PL/I program, which makes change for an amount DIFF dollars, using $20 bills and smaller denominations. The example is supposed to handle positive values of DIFF up to $10,000; the part we have omitted deals with negative and zero values.

```
     DECLARE A(8) REAL DECIMAL FIXED(6,2) INITIAL(20.,10.,5.,1.,.25,
     .1,.05,.01),(AMT_PD,DIFF,COST) REAL DECIMAL FIXED(8,2),
     (I,J,NT) REAL DECIMAL FIXED(3);
 ...

     CHANGE:DO I=1 TO 8;
         NT=0;
         CASH:DO J=1 TO 50;

/* IN THIS LOOP WE DETERMINE THE MAXIMUM NUMBERS OF TIMES THE
   DIFFERENCE IS DIVISIBLE BY THE I(TH) DENOMINATION    */

             IF DIFF/(J*A(I))<1 THEN GO TO OUT;
             NT=J;
         END CASH;
/*  WE THEN DECREASE THE DIFFERENCE BY THE APPROPRIATE AMOUNT
    AND PRINT THE APPROPRIATE STATEMENT       */

         OUT:IF NT>0 THEN DO;
         DIFF=DIFF−NT*A(I);
         IF I=1 THEN
             PUT SKIP(2) LIST(NT,'TWENTY DOLLAR BILLS');
         IF I=2 THEN
             PUT SKIP(2) LIST(NT,'TEN DOLLAR BILLS');
```

continued on next page

31

```
 IF  I=3 THEN
        PUT SKIP(2) LIST(NT,'FIVE DOLLAR BILLS');
 IF  I=4 THEN
        PUT SKIP(2) LIST(NT,'ONE DOLLAR BILLS');
 IF  I=5 THEN
        PUT SKIP(2) LIST(NT,'QUARTERS');
 IF  I=6 THEN
        PUT SKIP(2) LIST(NT,'DIMES');
 IF  I=7 THEN
        PUT SKIP(2) LIST(NT,'NICKELS');
 IF  I=8 THEN
        PUT SKIP(2) LIST(NT,'PENNIES');
 END CHANGE;
```

Consider the variable NT. It always has the value J−1 whenever it is referenced; it is not needed. Worse, its presence helps obscure an important point — the algorithm is wrong.

The inner DO loop (at label CASH) is clearly designed to exit via the IF before the loop completes. But 50 times $20 is only $1000, not $10,000, so an exit can occur from the bottom of the loop. The program will make change poorly at or over $1020, and incorrectly over $1820.50.

Whenever a DO loop is designed "never" to exit normally, one should ask:

1) Are there any circumstances when a normal exit might take place?

2) What happens if such an exit does occur?

The first question points to the typo that made the upper limit of the CASH loop 50 instead of 500; the second question reveals that the program charges straight on after an error. (A judiciously placed error message, plus a comprehensive set of test cases, would have brought this bug to light before it became a bad example.)

You might ask if it's fair to criticize such a "typographical" error, as we have done several times. Our answer is that, regrettably, a program with a typo in it won't work. If you're lucky, it will fail to compile. Worse, like this one, it may run but provide subtly wrong answers.

One flaw in a program is often a clue that more are present; that applies here. The whole purpose of the strange computation in the CASH loop is to determine the maximum number of times the Ith denomination A(I) can be removed from DIFF without causing overdraw. This is exactly what division does. In fact, DIFF/A(I) gives the desired result when truncated to the next lower integer, and the built-in function FLOOR performs just such a truncation. The CASH loop is not only incorrect, but wasteful and unnecessary.

Let us reconsider the data representation. It hardly seems necessary to rattle down a series of IFs to output the appropriate denomination name. If instead we use indexing, we can rewrite the fragment as:

```
DECLARE NAME(8) CHARACTER(19) INITIAL(
          'TWENTY DOLLAR BILLS', 'TEN DOLLAR BILLS   ',
          'FIVE DOLLAR BILLS  ', 'ONE DOLLAR BILLS   ',
          'QUARTERS           ', 'DIMES              ',
          'NICKELS            ', 'PENNIES            ');
DECLARE DENOM(8) REAL DECIMAL FIXED (6,2)
          INITIAL(20.00, 10.00, 5.00, 1.00,
                   0.25,  0.10, 0.05, 0.01);
DECLARE NT REAL DECIMAL FIXED (3);
DECLARE DIFF REAL DECIMAL FIXED (8,2);
  ...

  DO I = 1 TO 8;
     NT = FLOOR(DIFF/DENOM(I));
     DIFF = MOD(DIFF, DENOM(I));
     IF NT>0 THEN PUT SKIP(2) LIST (NT, NAME(I));
  END;
```

The different denomination names are collected into a character-string array NAME so we can use the computed index NT to select the one to print. NT now performs a useful function and so is retained. Not only is this version smaller and more readable, but it works correctly for any positive value that DIFF can assume. (We have not shown the code for the case when DIFF is negative or zero.)

It is interesting that this program failed to use truncating division when it should have, while the very first example in Chapter 1 used it to excess. In either case, the result is obscure code. Some friendly criticism could have helped each toward a happier middle ground. (Curiously, manuscripts are almost always reviewed before publication, yet programs are most often inspected only by the original coder and the compiler. Both have blind spots.)

Use data arrays to avoid repetitive control sequences.

It is easy to overlook a poor choice of data representation by getting involved in fixing up the intricate code that usually accompanies it. The following program reads cards and centers the non-blank information on each card within a border of periods.

```
      DIMENSION STRING(80),PHRASE(80)
      BLANK = 1H
      PERIOD = 1H.
  999 READ 100, (PHRASE(I),I=1,80)
  100 FORMAT(80A1)
  103 FORMAT(1H0)
C
C     LOOP 1
C
      NBEF=0
      J =1
    1 IF(PHRASE(J).NE.BLANK) GO TO 2
      NBEF=NBEF+1
      J = J+1
      IF(J.EQ.81) GO TO 1000
      GO TO 1
C
C     LOOP 2
C
    2 NAFT=0
      I=80
    3 IF(PHRASE(I).NE.BLANK)GO TO 4
      NAFT=NAFT+1
      I=I-1
      GO TO 3
C
C     COMPUTE LENGTHS OF PHRASE AND MARGIN
C
    4 LENGTH=80-(NBEF+NAFT)
      MARGIN = (80-LENGTH)/2+1
      IND1=NBEF
      IND2=MARGIN
      DO 41 J=2,79
   41 STRING(J)=BLANK
C
C     TRANSFER PHRASE TO STRING
C
      DO 5 I=1,LENGTH
      IND1=IND1+1
      IND2=IND2+1
    5 STRING(IND2) = PHRASE(IND1)
      STRING(1)=PERIOD
      STRING(80) = PERIOD
      PRINT 103
      PRINT 101,(STRING(I),I=1,80)
  101 FORMAT(1H , 80(1H.)/3(2H .,78X,1H./),1H ,80A1/3(2H .,78X,1H./)
     1,1H ,80(1H.))
      GO TO 999
 1000 PRINT 102
  102 FORMAT(1X, 37HBLANK CARD READ IN. EXIT FROM CENTER.)
      CALL EXIT
      END
```

Let us first examine the two errors that mar this otherwise straightforward program. The loop that ends at statement 5 copies the non-blank part of PHRASE into the appropriate part of STRING. Then positions 1 and 80 of the output area, STRING, are overwritten with a PERIOD, regardless of the length of the input. This bodes ill for input strings 79 or 80 characters long. We can avoid the overwrite by putting the two statements that set STRING(1) and STRING(80) before the loop, although it might be better to widen the output format to print 82 columns instead.

The second bug is more serious. We will leave it as an exercise for the reader to verify that even-length input fields are not centered, but are placed one position too far to the right. When the length is 80, this causes overwriting of STRING(81), which of course is not defined.

Rather than trying to patch the errors, let us re-examine the data structure. A moment of study reveals that two arrays, PHRASE and STRING, are used to hold only one set of data, the original input card. We can eliminate this double representation by reading the input into the middle of one big array of blanks, then writing out the appropriate part with the right number of blanks on each end.

With this organization, the code writes itself:

```
      INTEGER PHRASE(160), BLANK
      DATA BLANK /' '/
      DO 50 I = 1,160
         PHRASE(I) = BLANK
   50 CONTINUE
C
  100 READ(5,101) (PHRASE(I), I = 41,120)
  101 FORMAT(80A1)
C            LNB=LEFTMOST NON-BLANK, IRNB=RIGHTMOST
      LNB = 0
      DO 200 I = 41,120
         IF (PHRASE(I).NE.BLANK) IRNB = I
         IF (LNB.EQ.0 .AND. PHRASE(I).NE.BLANK) LNB = I
  200 CONTINUE
      IF (LNB .EQ. 0) GOTO 1000
      IRIGHT = (79+IRNB+LNB)/2
      LEFT = IRIGHT-79
      WRITE(6,201) (PHRASE(I), I = LEFT,IRIGHT)
  201    FORMAT(1X, 82('.'), /,
     $         3(1X, '.', 80X, '.', /),
     $         1X, '.', 80A1, '.', /,
     $         3(1X, '.', 80X, '.', /),
     $         1X, 82('.') )
      GOTO 100
C
 1000 WRITE(6,1001)
 1001 FORMAT(1X, 'BLANK CARD READ IN. EXIT FROM CENTER.')
      STOP
      END
```

The actual centering part is now smaller by a factor of three, and that much simpler. As a fringe benefit, it is correct. (This problem is easier in PL/I because variables are permitted in format statements. Try it.)

Choosing a better data structure is often an art, which we cannot teach. Often you must write a preliminary draft of the code before you can determine what changes in the data structure will help simplify control. The place to begin such improvements is by asking, "How can I structure the data so the computation becomes as nearly trivial as possible?"

Choose a data representation
that makes the program simple.

Let us turn now to flow of control. Decision-making statements can come so thick and fast as to obscure the final goals, as in this quadratic equation solver:

```
C      OBTAINS SOLUTIONS OF THE EQUATION A*X**2 + B*X + C = 0
C
    10 READ(5,8000) A,B,C
  8000 FORMAT(3F10.5)
C      A IN COLUMNS 1-10, B IN COLUMNS 11-20, C IN COLUMNS 21-30
       WRITE(6,9000) A,B,C
  9000 FORMAT(4H0A = F12.5,3X,3HB = ,F12.5,3X,3HC = ,F12.5)
C      TEST FOR TWO ZEROS
       IF(B.EQ.0..AND.C.EQ.0.)  GO TO 15
C      AT THIS POINT EITHER B, OR C, OR BOTH MAY BE NONZERO
       IF(B.NE.0..AND.C.NE.0.)  GO TO 50
C      AT THIS POINT EITHER B IS 0 OR C IS ZERO
       IF(A) 30,20,30
    15 IF(A.EQ.0.) STOP
    20 WRITE(6,9010)
  9010 FORMAT(33H TRIVIAL CASE. TWO OR MORE ZEROS.)
       GO TO 10
C      NOW TEST FOR C = 0 CASE.
    30 IF(C)  60,40,60
    40 XA = B/A
       XB = 0.
       GO TO 100
    50 IF(A.NE.0.)  GO TO 60
       XA = -C/B
       XB = 0.
       GO TO 100
C      START OF MAIN COMPUTATION
    60 Q = B*B-4.*A*C
       XX = -B/(2.*A)
       IF(Q)  80,70,80
    70 XA = XX
       XB = XX
       GO TO 100
    80 QA = ABS(Q)
       XS = SQRT(QA)/(2.*A)
       IF(Q) 110,110,90
    90 XA = XX + XS
       XB = XX - XS
```

continued on next page

```
  100 WRITE(6,9020) XA,XB
 9020 FORMAT(5H X1 = ,F12.5,3X,4HX2 = ,F12.5)
      GO TO 10
  110 XA = XS
      XB = -XS
      WRITE(6,9030) XX,XA,XX,XB
 9030 FORMAT(5H X1 = ,F12.5,2H + ,F12.5,2H I,5X,4HX2 = ,F12.5,2H +,
     1 F12.5,2H I)
      GO TO 10
      END
```

A painful trace through the logic reveals several small errors. The most significant is statement 40, the case where only C=0, which should have a minus sign:

```
   40 XA = -B/A
```

Statement 20 writes "TRIVIAL CASE. TWO OR MORE ZEROS.", even though the case where all three coefficients are zero is eliminated by the STOP at statement 15. Worse, the same message is delivered for the equations

(1) $A*X**2 = 0$, a valid equation with a double root at zero.

(2) $B*X = 0$, which has a single root at zero.

(3) $C = 0$, which is true only when C is zero.

Trivial they may be, but all are different and two out of the three are legitimate. Finally, for the case where only A is zero, the program prints out two roots, $-C/B$ and 0.0, even though the equation has only one root.

A useful way to write a complex program is to code it first in a convenient, expressive pseudo-language (typically *not* Fortran or PL/I) and then, when it appears correct, to translate it into the language at hand (Fortran in this case). Thus for solving quadratic equations, we might write:

```
Read: read and print A,B,C
      if A=0 & B=0
          equation is C=0;  goto Read
      if A=0
          only root is -C/B;  goto Read
      if C=0
          roots are -B/A and 0;  goto Read
      Realpart = -B/(2A)
      Discrim = B**2-4AC
      D2 = sqrt(abs(Discrim))/(2A)
      if Discrim>=0
          roots are Realpart+D2 and Realpart-D2
      else
          roots are (Realpart,i*D2) and (Realpart,-i*D2)
      goto Read
```

Indeed this is no language in particular, but it is sufficiently precise for our needs, and readily understood. Now we translate. Since most Fortrans do not allow grouping of statements, let alone a PL/I-like IF–THEN–ELSE, we must link up the pieces of the IF–THEN–ELSE structures by GOTOs. At the same time we can fix minor details like output formats and statement labels, and make the variable names more mnemonic. The resulting code:

```
C      OBTAINS SOLUTIONS OF THE EQUATION A*X**2 + B*X + C = 0
C
   100 READ(5,101) A, B, C
   101 FORMAT (3F10.0)
       WRITE(6,102) A, B, C
   102 FORMAT ('0A =', 1PE16.6, '   B =', 1PE16.6, '   C =', 1PE16.6)
       IF (A .NE. 0.0 .OR. B .NE. 0.0) GOTO 200
          WRITE(6,103) C
   103    FORMAT (' EQUATION SAYS', 1PE16.6,' = 0')
          GOTO 100
   200 IF (A .NE. 0.0) GOTO 300
          R1 = -C/B
          WRITE(6,201) R1
   201    FORMAT (' ONE ROOT. R =', 1PE16.6)
          GOTO 100
C                                         A IS NOT ZERO
   300 IF (C .NE. 0.0) GOTO 400
          R1 = -B/A
          R2 = 0.0
          WRITE(6,301) R1, R2
   301    FORMAT (' R1 =', 1PE16.6, '   R2 =', 1PE16.6)
          GOTO 100
C                                         GENERAL CASE: A,C NON-ZERO
   400 RREAL = -B/(2.0*A)
       DISC = B**2 - 4.0*A*C
       RIMAG = SQRT(ABS(DISC))/(2.0*A)
       IF (DISC .LT. 0.0) GOTO 500
          R1 = RREAL + RIMAG
          R2 = RREAL - RIMAG
          WRITE(6,301) R1, R2
          GOTO 100
   500 R1 = -RIMAG
       WRITE(6,501) RREAL, RIMAG, RREAL, R1
   501 FORMAT (' R1 = (', 1PE16.6, ',', 1PE16.6, ')',
      $    '    R2 = (', 1PE16.6, ',', 1PE16.6, ')')
       GOTO 100
       END
```

Two roots are printed only when there are two, one is printed when and only when there is one, and an imaginary part is printed only when called for. More important, it is easier to determine how the program gets to each separate case. (This program is still far from being a general-purpose quadratic-equation solver; the defenses needed against every conceivable numerical hazard require more analysis than we can go into here.)

Write first in an easy-to-understand pseudo-language;
then translate into whatever language you have to use.

IF—THEN—ELSE constructions formed the framework of our quadratic routine, as they do in most programs. But mere use of IF—THEN—ELSE does not guarantee that the result will stand up. Consider this fragment, which computes the effective weight of an airplane, based on its true weight, length, and wingspan.

```
IF LENGTH >= 30 & LENGTH <= 50 THEN

    IF WING < .6*LENGTH THEN WEIGHT1 =
    (1+.08-.037)*WEIGHT;

    ELSE WEIGHT1=(1+.08+.045)*WEIGHT;
ELSE   IF LENGTH > 50 & LENGTH < 60 THEN

        IF WING < .6*LENGTH THEN
        WEIGHT1=(1+.09-.037)*
        WEIGHT;

        ELSE WEIGHT1=(1+.09+.045)*
        WEIGHT;

    ELSE   IF LENGTH > 60 & LENGTH
            < 80 THEN

    IF   WING < .6*LENGTH THEN
            WEIGHT1=(1+.105-.037)*
            WEIGHT;

    ELSE WEIGHT1=(1+.105+.045)*
            WEIGHT;

            ELSE IF WING < .6*LENGTH
                 THEN

                WEIGHT1=(1+.122-
                .037)*WEIGHT;
                ELSE WEIGHT1=(1+
                .122+.045)*WEIGHT;
```

When a program is well-structured, its layout can be made clean. For instance, programs that avoid labels and undisciplined branches can often use indentation to emphasize the logical structure. (This program was originally displayed with vertical bars joining IFs with their corresponding ELSEs.) But indentation is no substitute for organization; tasteful formatting and top-to-bottom flow is no guarantee that the code cannot be improved. The entire structure is turned inside out. If the test on WING is done first and the result saved for later use, and if we remove all the redundant tests, the code simplifies remarkably. Rearrangement also reveals the oversight in the original that omitted the case where LENGTH is exactly 60.

```
IF WING < 0.6*LENGTH
    THEN CORR = 1.0 - 0.037;
    ELSE CORR = 1.0 + 0.045;

IF LENGTH<30
    THEN ;   /* NOT SPECIFIED IN ORIGINAL */
ELSE IF LENGTH<=50
    THEN WEIGHT1 = (CORR+0.08)*WEIGHT;
ELSE IF LENGTH<=60
    THEN WEIGHT1 = (CORR+0.09)*WEIGHT;
ELSE IF LENGTH<80
    THEN WEIGHT1 = (CORR+0.105)*WEIGHT;
ELSE
        WEIGHT1 = (CORR+0.122)*WEIGHT;
```

Both versions use a nest of IF—THEN—ELSEs, but ours uses it in a special way: we never use an IF inside the THEN, but only in the ELSE. The result is much easier to understand, because we know that exactly one case is done, and it is clear how we get to it: it is the first condition satisfied as we read down the list of ELSE IFs. After one of these has been done, execution resumes after the entire statement. Some languages have a "CASE" statement that expresses this construction directly; in PL/I we use a well-behaved IF—THEN—ELSE, and in Fortran a carefully chosen set of IFs and GOTOs, as in the quadratic equation solver. (The computed GOTO in Fortran can also implement an efficient CASE statement in some circumstances; all CASEs should end by branching to a common point.)

Use IF...ELSE IF...ELSE IF...ELSE...
to implement multi-way branches.

A good way to confuse things is simply to try to use the minimum possible number of IFs. This subroutine generates simple moves (no jumps) for a checker-playing program. The routine tries to make up to four moves: forward right and left, backward right and left. If the move is off the board or to an occupied square, it is disallowed. White men may only move forward and black men may only move backward. Kings may move either way.

```
          SUBROUTINE SEARCH (BOARD,I,J,MOVROW,MOVCOL,L)
          DIMENSION BOARD(8,8),MOVROW(4),MOVCOL(4)
          INTEGER BOARD
C         ASSUME THE CHECKERS ARE CODED AS FOLLOWS:
C             1—WHITE MAN
C               2—WHITE KING
C                 3—BLACK MAN
C                   4—BLACK KING
C         BOARD IS THE ARRAY REPRESENTING THE
C         CHECKER BOARD WITH 0'S IN POSITIONS WITH
C         NO MEN, I AND J ARE THE COORDINATES OF
C         THE MAN WHOSE MOVES ARE BEING SEARCHED
C         FOR, MOVROW AND MOVCOL ARE ARRAYS WHICH
C         ARE TO CONTAIN THE ROW AND COLUMN COORDINATES
C         OF POSSIBLE MOVES AND L COUNTS THE NUMBER OF
C         POSSIBLE MOVES ***
C         IF(BOARD(I,J) IS ZERO, ERROR HAS BEEN MADE
          IF(BOARD(I,J).EQ.0) STOP
          L=0
          K=BOARD(I,J)
C         ASSUME WHITE MEN START IN ROWS ONE
C         TO THREE, BLACK MEN IN ROWS SIX TO EIGHT.....
          GO TO (4,4,6,4),K
C         ENTRY FOR ALL EXCEPT BLACK MAN
C         FORWARD RIGHT
C         TEST IF MOVE IS ON BOARD
        4 IF(I.EQ.8) GO TO 8
          IF(J.EQ.8) GO TO 2
          IF(BOARD(I+1,J+1).NE.0) GO TO 2
          L=L+1
          MOVROW(L)=I+1
          MOVCOL(L)=J+1
C         FORWARD LEFT
        2 IF(J.EQ.1) GO TO 8
          IF(BOARD(I+1,J-1).NE.0) GO TO 8
          L=L+1
          MOVROW(L)=I+1
          MOVCOL(L)=J-1
C         EXIT TEST FOR WHITE MAN
        8 IF(K.EQ.1) RETURN
C         BACKWARD RIGHT
        6 IF(I.EQ.1) RETURN
          IF(J.EQ.8) GO TO 10
          IF(BOARD(I-1,J+1).NE.0) GO TO 10
          L=L+1
          MOVROW(L)=I-1
          MOVCOL(L)=J+1
C         BACKWARD LEFT
       10 IF(J.EQ.1) RETURN
          IF(BOARD(I-1,J-1).NE.0) RETURN
          L=L+1
          MOVROW(L)=I-1
          MOVCOL(L)=J-1
          RETURN
          END
```

Again, the repeated tests, with no obvious pattern, should alert us to a possible structural weakness. Some combination of statements ought surely to be isolated as a second subroutine, to modularize the code. If we do not fret over making a few "unnecessary" tests, we can unsnarl the tangle of branches with a general "test and store" subroutine, which decides whether one specified direction represents a legal move, and saves it. All that is left then is the constraint on what men may make certain moves, which can be simply encoded:

```
      SUBROUTINE SEARCH(BOARD, I, J, ROW, COL, L)
      INTEGER BOARD(8,8), ROW(4), COL(4)
C            BOARD(I,J)=0 => EMPTY SQUARE
C                        1 => WHITE MAN, 2 => WHITE KING
C                        3 => BLACK MAN, 4 => BLACK KING
C            I INCREASES FORWARD, J INCREASES RIGHT
C            L COUNTS THE MOVES
      IF (I.LT.1 .OR. I.GT.8 .OR. J.LT.1 .OR. J.GT.8)
     $    CALL ERROR(1)
      K = BOARD(I,J)
      IF (K.LT.1 .OR. K.GT.4) CALL ERROR(2)
      L = 0
      IF (K.NE.3) CALL STORE(BOARD, I+1, J+1, ROW, COL, L)
      IF (K.NE.3) CALL STORE(BOARD, I+1, J-1, ROW, COL, L)
      IF (K.NE.1) CALL STORE(BOARD, I-1, J+1, ROW, COL, L)
      IF (K.NE.1) CALL STORE(BOARD, I-1, J-1, ROW, COL, L)
      RETURN
      END

      SUBROUTINE STORE(BOARD, IC, JC, ROW, COL, L)
      INTEGER BOARD(8,8), ROW(4), COL(4)
      IF (IC.LT.1 .OR. IC.GT.8 .OR. JC.LT.1 .OR. JC.GT.8) RETURN
      IF (BOARD(IC,JC).NE.0) RETURN
      L = L+1
      ROW(L) = IC
      COL(L) = JC
      RETURN
      END
```

Separating code into appropriate modules is an important aspect of structuring a program. As we can see here, the subroutine call permits us to summarize the *irregularities* in the argument list, where we can see quickly what is going on. The subroutine itself summarizes the *regularities* of the code, so repeated patterns need not be used. An added advantage of this version is that including complexities like jumps later on will be rather easy. "Optimizing" too early in the life of a program can kill its chances for growth.

We have included calls to an unspecified error-printing routine, to simplify the handling of illegal inputs. Such a subroutine can overcome the inertia normally felt when it comes time to check for possible errors. Conventional wisdom says that the calls to ERROR should be inserted "until the program is debugged," then removed. Leave them in indefinitely — the insurance is cheap.

Modularize.   Use subroutines.

Excessive use of labels (statement numbers) and GOTOs is often the hallmark of undisciplined design. Tracing flow of control can be next to impossible if there are too many potential paths from one point to another. Even when such code is correct, it is hard to understand and thus even harder to modify. Consider this program for converting a year and day of the year into the month and day of the month:

```
DATES:    PROC OPTIONS (MAIN);
READ:     GET DATA (IYEAR, IDATE);
          IF IDATE < 1 | IDATE > 366 | IYEAR < 0 THEN RETURN;
          IF IDATE <= 31 THEN GO TO JAN;
          L = 1;
          I = IYEAR/400; IF I = IYEAR/400 THEN GO TO LEAP;
          I = IYEAR/100; IF I = IYEAR/100 THEN GO TO NOLEAP;
          I = IYEAR/4; IF I = IYEAR/4 THEN GO TO LEAP;
NOLEAP:   L = 0;
          IF IDATE > 365 THEN RETURN;
  LEAP:   IF IDATE > 181 + L THEN GO TO G181;
          IF IDATE > 90 + L THEN GO TO G90;
          IF IDATE > 59 + L THEN GO TO G59;
          MONTH = 2; IDAY = IDATE - 31; GO TO OUT;
   G59:   MONTH = 3; IDAY = IDATE - (59 + L); GO TO OUT;
   G90:   IF IDATE > 120 + L THEN GO TO G120;
          MONTH = 4; IDAY = IDATE - (90 + L); GO TO OUT;
  G120:   IF IDATE > 151 + L THEN GO TO G151;
          MONTH = 5; IDAY = IDATE - (120 + L); GO TO OUT;
  G151:   MONTH = 6; IDAY = IDATE - (151 + L); GO TO OUT;
  G181:   IF IDATE > 273 + L THEN GO TO G273;
          IF IDATE > 243 + L THEN GO TO G243;
          IF IDATE > 212 + L THEN GO TO G212;
          MONTH = 7; IDAY = IDATE - (181 + L); GO TO OUT;
  G212:   MONTH = 8; IDAY = IDATE - (212 + L); GO TO OUT;
  G243:   MONTH = 9; IDAY = IDATE - (243 + L); GO TO OUT;
  G273:   IF IDATE > 334 + L THEN GO TO G334;
          IF IDATE > 304 + L THEN GO TO G304;
          MONTH = 10; IDAY = IDATE - (273 + L); GO TO OUT;
  G304:   MONTH = 11; IDAY = IDATE - (304 + L); GO TO OUT;
  G334:   MONTH = 12; IDAY = IDATE - (334 + L);
  OUT:    PUT DATA (MONTH,IDAY,IYEAR) SKIP;
          GO TO READ;
  JAN:    MONTH=1; IDAY=IDATE; GO TO OUT;
          END DATES;
```

We have nothing to say about the "structure" of this program; the code speaks for itself. There is one curious usage that bears explaining, however, in the leap year determination. Three lines have the form

```
I = IYEAR/n;  IF I = IYEAR/n THEN GO TO label;
```

It would seem that the GOTO is always obeyed, since I surely equals that which was just assigned to it. But in PL/I this is not necessarily so. In the assignment any fractional part is discarded, but in the comparison it is retained. The code thus tests whether IYEAR/n is an integer and branches if it is. Try to explain that to a novice programmer. Such unobvious code should surely be replaced by

```
IF MOD(IYEAR,n)=0 THEN GOTO label;
```

This still may not be obvious to a rank beginner, but it is unambiguous and easily learned.

Calendar computations are notoriously complex, but the approach shown above makes them seem even worse. All of the information about how many days precede the first of each month should be put in a table instead of being strung throughout the code. Then a more organized approach is possible. When undertaking anything complicated, we heed some advice from *Alice in Wonderland:*

> The White Rabbit put on his spectacles. "Where shall I be-
> gin, please your Majesty?" he asked.
> "Begin at the beginning," the King said, very gravely, "and
> go on till you come to the end: then stop."

Applying this principle gives:

```
DATES: PROCEDURE OPTIONS (MAIN);
    DECLARE NDAYS(0:1,0:12) INITIAL(
        0,31,59,90,120,151,181,212,243,273,304,334,365,  /* NON-LEAP */
        0,31,60,91,121,152,182,213,244,274,305,335,366); /* LEAP */

READ:
    GET LIST (IYEAR, IDATE) COPY;

    IF MOD(IYEAR,400)=0 |
        (MOD(IYEAR,100)¬=0 & MOD(IYEAR,4)=0)
            THEN LEAP = 1;
            ELSE LEAP = 0;

    IF IYEAR<1753 | IYEAR>3999 | IDATE<=0 | IDATE>NDAYS(LEAP,12) THEN
    DO; PUT SKIP LIST('BAD YEAR, DATE -', IYEAR, IDATE);
        GOTO READ;
    END;
```

continued on next page

```
      DO MO = 1 TO 12;
        IF IDATE<=NDAYS(LEAP,MO) THEN
            DO; PUT SKIP LIST(MO, IDATE-NDAYS(LEAP,MO-1), IYEAR);
                GOTO READ;
            END;
      END;
   END DATES;
```

We begin at the beginning (with a simple data structure), go on (by deciding if we have a leap year or not, and whether the date is valid), until we come to the end (by printing either a valid date or the invalid input), then stop. We have reduced the fifteen internal labels to one, and the 26 GOTOs to two, by using only the patterns described above. Since a branch can occur only to a label, we have that much less to worry about.

Use GOTOs only to implement a fundamental structure.

Some programmers argue that the GOTO statement should be eliminated completely. This is not usually possible in Fortran or convenient in PL/I; we are content when we can identify the role of each GOTO in implementing the basic structures. Our programs contain GOTOs, but they are used in a stylized, disciplined way, implementing some basic program structure like IF—THEN—ELSE.

The DATES program above, for instance, is basically an "infinite" loop (which exits when the input is exhausted). The two GOTOs say "skip the remaining steps of this case and *loop* back to the top." In some languages, an explicit LOOP statement is available; in Fortran and PL/I, LOOP is often best written with a label and a GOTO.

Fewer GOTOs are needed in PL/I programs, however, if more use is made of the WHILE clause in the DO statement and the ELSE part of IF—THEN—ELSE. The infinite READ loop in our version above, for instance, could be rendered as

```
      DO WHILE ('1'B);
         ...
      END;
```

or as

```
      DO NREAD = 0 BY 0;
         ...
      END;
```

The IF that tests for an invalid year could be augmented by an ELSE that does the computation if the date is valid, and the determination of the correct month could be done by another WHILE (which controls the execution of a null statement). The result contains no GOTOs:

```
DATES: PROCEDURE OPTIONS (MAIN);
    DECLARE NDAYS(0:1,0:12) INITIAL(
       0,31,59,90,120,151,181,212,243,273,304,334,365,   /* NON-LEAP */
       0,31,60,91,121,152,182,213,244,274,305,335,366); /* LEAP */

    DO WHILE('1'B);
       GET LIST (IYEAR, IDATE) COPY;

       IF MOD(IYEAR,400)=0 |
          (MOD(IYEAR,100)¬=0 & MOD(IYEAR,4)=0)
             THEN LEAP = 1;
             ELSE LEAP = 0;

       IF IYEAR<1753 | IYEAR>3999 | IDATE<=0 | IDATE>NDAYS(LEAP,12)
          THEN PUT SKIP LIST('BAD YEAR, DATE -', IYEAR, IDATE);

       ELSE DO;
          DO MO = 1 TO 12 WHILE (IDATE>NDAYS(LEAP,MO));
          END;

          PUT SKIP LIST(MO, IDATE-NDAYS(LEAP,MO-1), IYEAR);
       END;
    END;
END DATES;
```

Which is better? Both versions are clear, simple, and straightforward. The answer depends on personal taste.

Avoid GOTOs completely if you can keep the program readable.

One way to gain a real appreciation for proper control structures is to look at a large program that uses almost none of them. The following program simulates a mouse trying to find a path through a maze by the simple rule, "Turn right if you can, left if you must." The maze is a Boolean matrix, with ones representing possible paths. A path consists of a connected series of horizontal and vertical strings of ones that enters the maze somewhere and exits somewhere else. Remember that a big program should be a collection of manageable pieces, each of which must obey the rules of good style.

```
EX510:PROCEDURE OPTIONS(MAIN);

  /*   FIRST ASSUME MAXIMUM DIMENSIONS FOR THE MAZE  -  HERE 50 X 50    */
  DCL (POINT(2,60),X,Y,(POSITIONX,POSITIONY)(2500)) DEC FIXED(4),
       MAZE(50,50) BIT(1),XMAZE(50,50) CHAR(1) ,
       BRANCH LABEL(LOOKL,LOOKR,LOOKU,LOOKD);
       XMAZE='X';
  GET LIST(N,M);

  GET EDIT(((MAZE(I,J) DO J=1 TO N) DO I=1 TO M))(COLUMN(1),(N)B(1));
  PUT EDIT(((MAZE(I,J) DO J=1 TO N) DO I=1 TO M))(LINE(33-M/2),
       (M) (COLUMN(40-N/2),(N) B(1),SKIP));
```

continued on next page

```
      I,MM,NN=1;          II,IN1,IN2=0;

 /*  NEXT FIND A PATH THROUGH THE MAZE  —  THIS IS DONE BY SIMULATING
A MAN KEEPING HIS RIGHT HAND IN CONTACT WITH THE WALL AND FOLLOWING IT  */

      RUNUD:DO K1=NN TO N BY N-1;
           DO K2=IN1+1 TO M;
            IF MAZE(K2,K1)='1'B THEN GO TO TEST1;
      END RUNUD;

      RUNLR:DO K1=MM TO M BY M-1;
           DO K2=IN2 TO N;
            IF MAZE(K1,K2)='1'B THEN GO TO TEST2;
      END RUNLR;

      TEST1:X,NN=K2;            POSITIONX(1)=X;
            Y,IN1=K1;           POSITIONY(1)=Y;
            IF NN=1 THEN GO TO LOOKR;
                      GO TO LOOKL;

      TEST2:Y,MM=K2;            POSITIONY(1)=Y;
            X,IN2=K1;           POSITIONX(1)=X;
            IF MM=1 THEN GO TO LOOKD;

         LOOKU:IF MAZE(X-1,Y)='1'B THEN DO;
               BRANCH=LOOKR;         X=X-1;
                 GO TO SET;
                                END;

         LOOKL:IF MAZE(X,Y-1)='1'B THEN DO ;
               BRANCH=LOOKU;         Y=Y-1;
                 GO TO SET;
                                     END;

         LOOKD:IF MAZE(X+1,Y)='1'B THEN DO;
               BRANCH=LOOKL;         X=X+1;
                 GO TO SET;
                                END;

         LOOKR:IF MAZE(X,Y+1)='1'B THEN DO;
               BRANCH=LOOKD;         Y=Y+1;
                 GO TO SET;
                                END;
                                ELSE GO TO LOOKU;

         SET:I=I+1;

         POSITIONX(I)=X;              POSITIONY(I)=Y;

      IF X<N&X>1&Y<M&Y>1 THEN GO TO BRANCH;

      IF X=POSITIONX(1)&Y=POSITIONY(1) THEN DO;
              IF IN2=0 THEN GO TO RUNUD;
                   ELSE GO TO RUNLR;
                                 END;

 /*  NOW PICK OUT THOSE PARTS OF THE PATH FOLLOWED WHICH WENT IN A LOOP OR
        DEAD ENDED   */

 /* NOTE THE TRANSFER STATEMENT WHICH CAUSES A TRANSFER TO WHAT LOOKS
    LIKE THE NEXT STATEMENT  —  ACTUALLY THE COMPILER CREATES A DUMMY STATEMENT
    BETWEEN THESE TWO TO END THE INNER DO LOOP  —  HENCE  THE PROGRAM MUST
    BRANCH AROUND IT   */
```

continued on next page

```
      SORT:DO J=I TO 2 BY-1;
         DO K=J-1 TO 1 BY -1;
            IF POSITIONX(K)=POSITIONX(J)&POSITIONY(K)=POSITIONY(J)
                  THEN DO;         II=II+1;        POINT(1,II)=J;
                     POINT(2,II)=K;    J=K+1;      GO TO ENDSORT;
      ENDSORT:END SORT;

 /*  FINALLY SET UP THE FINAL MAZE WITH THE PATH FOLLOWED     */

      MERGE:DO KK=1 TO I;
            DO IK=1 TO II;
                  IF KK=POINT(2,IK) THEN KK=POINT(1,IK);
            END;

         XMAZE(POSITIONX(KK),POSITIONY(KK))=' ';
      END MERGE;
      PUT PAGE EDIT(((XMAZE(I,J) DO J=1 TO N) DO I=1 TO M))(LINE(33-M/2),
            (M) (COLUMN(40-N/2),(N) A(1),SKIP));

 END EX510;
```

The interesting thing about this program is that it successfully ran a test case, despite all the errors we are about to unearth. To debug this code by running test cases alone would clearly take a long time. Just proofreading is hard enough, because the control logic is so curiously distributed. Let us analyze the code by sections.

The DO loops at RUNUD and RUNLR inspect the borders of the maze, looking for an entrance. TEST1 and TEST2 start the mouse going "in" from an opening by transferring control to the appropriate LOOKx test. These implement the right-turn rule described above, either to find a path continuation or to cause the mouse to back out of a dead end. SET stores each point along the path and tests whether the mouse has reached the border again. If the mouse comes out where it went in, this is not a path, so the program goes back to the appropriate RUNxx DO loop to continue searching the border where it left off. Otherwise it falls through to the SORT and MERGE loops, which determine the path to be printed out.

The RUNxx DO loops have elaborate control parameters so that they can be resumed. This is not an easy thing to do, so we are not surprised to find that it is done wrong. At TEST1, for instance, we see that NN remembers the index K2; but at RUNUD, NN is associated with the index K1. Sure enough, the lower limits for all four DO loops are stored incorrectly. The program cannot properly resume the border scan.

There are other problems with these DO loops. If the maze has no entry points, or if there is no path through it, control falls through to TEST1 and the program starts looking around outside the array MAZE. (Remember what we said at the start of this chapter about DO loops that "never" terminate normally?) By definition, it is not possible to go "in" from a corner, yet each is tried and could give an uninteresting answer — a path that only runs along the edge. In fact, any adjacent ones on the border will be reported as a path. Finally, the two inner loops (on K2) are handled differently even though they perform similar functions. This tips us off that one of them is incorrect. (As a matter of fact both are, but the details are not worth pursuing.)

The four LOOKx tests form one of those repeated patterns we have already encountered several times. Defining the appropriate data structures should permit us to summarize all four tests in one. Then perhaps we could avoid the dubious GOTO BRANCH, which is a PL/I equivalent of Fortran's assigned GOTO and equally obscure. Anything that disguises flow of control should be avoided.

SORT and MERGE are correctly coded, but not well designed. It seems silly to save all the loops and dead ends encountered until the very end, when they can be readily eliminated along the way. Then it is not necessary to make a list of all the matching points so that loops can be skipped over on output. (POINT should be written as two arrays, by the way, and each should be much larger than 60 elements. POSITIONX and POSITIONY, on the other hand, need not be even half their current size of 2500.) SORT and MERGE are far more complicated than necessary.

Finally, the sequence

```
        GO TO ENDSORT;
    ENDSORT: END SORT;
```

is an open invitation to misunderstanding. The fact that a four line comment is needed to explain what is going on should be reason enough to rewrite the code. An even better reason is that the comment is wrong — *two* dummy statements are created to end *two* DO groups. How much easier and clearer it is to write

```
            GOTO ENDSORT;
        END;
    END;
ENDSORT: END SORT;
```

There are too many other errors to discuss in detail. An isolated border cell with value '1'B will cause grief, as will a non-square maze. Even for a maze as trivial as

```
000
111
000
```

the correct path is never found; when we ran it, after an indeterminate amount of poking around outside the maze the program reported that the middle cell on the left border forms a "path." When subscript range checking is turned on, the program aborts.

It is an enlightening exercise to patch the maze program, providing just enough corrections to permit it to handle reasonable inputs. But patching only serves to emphasize the shortcomings of this organization. After a brief attempt, most readers will agree that the best cure is not revision but a total rewrite.

Don't patch bad code — rewrite it.

Recasting the algorithm in terms of simple building blocks like IF—THEN—ELSE, DO—WHILE and subroutines gives:

```
/*    MOUSE IN A MAZE   */
/* SEARCHES PERIPHERY OF AN M X N MATRIX (MAX 50 X 50)   */
/* FOR AN ENTRY POINT.  THEN FOLLOWS PATH BY SIMULATING  */
/* MAN WITH RIGHT HAND ON WALL (TURN RIGHT IF YOU CAN,    */
/* LEFT IF YOU MUST) UNTIL HE REEMERGES.  FIRST PATH      */
/* WITH EXIT DIFFERENT THAN ENTRANCE IS ACCEPTED.         */
/* MAZE='1'B IS A PATH, MAZE='0'B IS A WALL.              */

EX510: PROCEDURE OPTIONS (MAIN);

/*** CONSTANTS ***/
    DECLARE (UP INITIAL(0), LEFT INITIAL(1),
             DOWN INITIAL(2), RIGHT INITIAL(3))
        STATIC FIXED BINARY;

/*** GLOBAL VARIABLES ***/
    DECLARE MAZE(50,50) BIT(1),
            (XPOS, YPOS)(1250) FIXED BINARY,
            L FIXED BINARY;

    ON ENDFILE STOP;

/*** INPUT AND LIST MAZE ***/
MORE:
    GET LIST (M, N);
    IF M<2 | M>50 | N<2 | N>50 THEN DO;
        PUT SKIP LIST (M, N, 'BAD DIMENSIONS');  STOP;
                                        END;

    GET EDIT (((MAZE(I,J) DO J = 1 TO N) DO I = 1 TO M))
        (COLUMN(1), (N)B(1));
    PUT PAGE EDIT (((MAZE(I,J) DO J = 1 TO N) DO I = 1 TO M))
        (LINE(33-M/2), (M)(COLUMN(40-N/2), (N)B(1)));

/*** SEARCH PERIPHERY ***/
    DECLARE FIND ENTRY (FIXED BINARY, FIXED BINARY, FIXED BINARY)
            RETURNS (BIT(1));       /* '1'B IF PATH FOUND */

    DO K = 2 TO M-1;
        IF FIND(K,1,RIGHT) THEN GOTO FOUND;
        IF FIND(K,N,LEFT)  THEN GOTO FOUND;
    END;
    DO K = 2 TO N-1;
        IF FIND(1,K,DOWN) THEN GOTO FOUND;
        IF FIND(M,K,UP)   THEN GOTO FOUND;
    END;

    PUT SKIP LIST ('NO ENTRANCE');  GOTO MORE;

/*** PRINT ANSWER ***/
    DECLARE XMAZE(50,50) CHARACTER(1);

FOUND:
```

continued on next page

```
        XMAZE = 'X';

        DO J = 1 TO L;          /* L, XPOS, YPOS ARE SET IN FIND */
            XMAZE(XPOS(J),YPOS(J)) = ' ';
        END;
        PUT PAGE EDIT (((XMAZE(I,J) DO J = 1 TO N) DO I = 1 TO M))
            (LINE(33-M/2), (M)(COLUMN(40-N/2), (N)A(1)));
        GOTO MORE;


/*  PROCEDURE FOR SEARCHING:  */
/*  BEGINS AT BORDER CELL KX,KY AND PROBES IN DIRECTION   */
/*  KW.  IF ENTRY THERE THEN FOLLOWS PATH, AND RETURNS    */
/*  '1'B IF COMES OUT SOMEWHERE ELSE.                     */
/*  STORES L ELEMENTS OF PATH IN XPOS, YPOS               */

    FIND: PROCEDURE (KX, KY, KW) RETURNS (BIT(1));

    /*** CONSTANTS ***/
        DECLARE (DX(0:3) INITIAL(-1,0,1,0), DY(0:3) INITIAL(0,-1,0,1))
            STATIC FIXED BINARY;

    /*** STORAGE ***/
        DECLARE (X, Y, W) FIXED BINARY;

        IF MAZE(KX,KY) = '0'B | MAZE(KX+DX(KW),KY+DY(KW)) = '0'B
            THEN RETURN ('0'B);

    /*** EXPLORE ***/
        XPOS(1) = KX;  YPOS(1) = KY;
        XPOS(2),X = KX+DX(KW);  YPOS(2),Y = KY+DY(KW);
        W = KW;  L = 2;

        DO WHILE (X>1 & X<M & Y>1 & Y<N);
            W = MOD(W+3,4);                         /* TURN RIGHT */

            DO WHILE (MAZE(X+DX(W),Y+DY(W)) = '0'B);
                W = MOD(W+1,4);         /* TURN LEFT UNTIL OUT */
            END;

            L = L+1;
            XPOS(L),X = X+DX(W);  YPOS(L),Y = Y+DY(W);

            DO J = L-2 TO 1 BY -1;                  /* TEST FOR KNOT */
                IF X = XPOS(J) & Y = YPOS(J) THEN
                    IF J = 1 THEN RETURN ('0'B);
                    ELSE DO;
                        L = J;  GOTO EXIT;
                        END;
        END;
    EXIT:
        END;

        RETURN ('1'B);                         /* REACHED BORDER */
    END FIND;

END EX510;
```

We use a sub-procedure FIND to do the actual searching. That way it is never necessary to go outside a DO loop and then try to continue it where it left off; instead the loop is exited early only when a solution is found. Moreover, we have isolated the path-hunting algorithm in a separate module, keeping it apart from the general control flow. Direction increments are encoded in the arrays DX and DY, so we can describe left and right turns in terms of modulus (wraparound) arithmetic on their subscripts. Loops in the path are eliminated as they are detected, so much less storage is needed.

The branch GOTO MORE which occurs several times in our code is of course a LOOP, which we have encountered before. The branch GOTO EXIT in the construction

```
DO J = L-2 TO 1 BY -1;                   /* TEST FOR KNOT */
  IF X = XPOS(J) & Y = YPOS(J) THEN
    IF J = 1 THEN RETURN ('0'B);
    ELSE DO;
      L = J;   GOTO EXIT;
      END;
  END;
EXIT:
```

is an example of another useful control structure, the BREAK, or early exit from a loop. Again, some languages provide a BREAK directly, but in PL/I and Fortran we are forced to more indirect ways of expressing it.

We decided to make the variables L, XPOS, and YPOS global, instead of passing them to FIND through the argument list. Ordinarily, it is best to use each variable in only a localized region of the program, to minimize the chance of conflicting usage. When argument lists become cumbersome, however, you must consider which variables are best made known to the entire program, that is, global. PL/I's EXTERNAL attribute and Fortran's COMMON statement make global variables known among parts of a program compiled as separate units. When you must use variables globally, comment the practice freely.

The maze program is pretty big; it takes a lot of effort to analyze. Our version is not smaller than the original, yet it is noticeably easier to read. There are about as many comments in each and the identifier names are essentially the same. The one main difference is structural.

We chose our control structures on the basis of legibility; people tend to understand them with little effort. Our version of the maze program has only three labels (other than procedure names). That in itself is no great accomplishment, but it indicates that the flow of control must be essentially from top to bottom. We thus have some assurance that we can read the program a small section at a time without much concern for the rest of the code. There is no other way to retain control of a large program.

Write and test a big program in small pieces.

Another tool for reducing apparent complexity is recursion. "Begin at the beginning," said the King of Hearts, but sometimes that does not seem possible. Converting an integer to a string of characters, for instance, must apparently be done backwards:

```
      SUBROUTINE ITOSTR(NUMB,KARS)
      DIMENSION KARS(20), KTEMPS(20)
      N = NUMB
      DO 1 I=1,20
      KTEMPS(I) = MOD(N,10) + 33B
      N = N/10
      IF (N.EQ.0) GOTO 2
    1 CONTINUE
      I = 20
    2 DO 3 J=1,I
    3 KARS(J) = KTEMPS(I+1-J)
      KARS(I+1) = 0
      RETURN
      END
```

This stores the decimal digits of NUMB right-to-left in KTEMPS, then copies them in reverse order into KARS.

The program fails, of course, when NUMB is negative. There is also a lurking bug, which would only surface on a computer that can represent integers to twenty decimal places. If I is equal to twenty as of statement 2, then the program will attempt to store a zero in KARS(21). The DIMENSION statement could be changed to cover this eventuality, but a better approach would delete KTEMPS and work directly in KARS; then there is no problem with the size of KTEMPS.

Adding 33B (presumably an octal constant for a specific machine) to convert a number to a character is extremely implementation dependent and should be avoided. It is better to output the KARS array in I1 format. This would be easier if we make ITOSTR a function, and return I, the location of the end of the string.

Our reason for showing this program, though, was to illustrate a valid use for recursion. Instead of saving up all the digits and reversing them we could write, in PL/I at least:

```
ITOSTR: PROCEDURE (NUMB, KARS);
   DECLARE KARS(*), I INITIAL(0);
   CALL ITOS(NUMB);  RETURN(I);

   ITOS: PROCEDURE(N) RECURSIVE;
      IF N>=10 THEN CALL ITOS(N/10);
      I = I+1;  KARS(I) = MOD(N,10);
      RETURN;
   END ITOS;
END ITOSTR;
```

We have left out code for negative numbers to keep the comparison reasonably direct. This version is conceptually simpler and requires no knowledge of how big a number can be. The procedure keeps calling itself with the trailing digit removed until it isolates the leading digit, then the digits are stored in KARS in proper order.

This represents no saving of time or storage. Somewhere in the computer must be maintained a list of all the places ITOSTR is called, so the program can eventually find its way back. But the storage for that list is shared among many different uses. More important, it is managed automatically and places no burden on the programmer.

Learning to think recursively takes some effort, but that is repaid with smaller and simpler programs. To handle negative numbers with ITOSTR, for instance, we need only change the initial call to ITOS to

```
IF NUMB<0 THEN
    DO;
        I = I+1;
        KARS(I) = -1;
    END;
CALL ITOS(ABS(NUMB));
```

and we return a negative digit in KARS(1) as a flag. Note how each section handles only a small part of the problem, then makes a recursive call when necessary to handle the rest.

Not every problem benefits from a recursive approach, but those that deal with data that is recursively defined often lead to very complicated programs unless the code is also recursive. A list, for example, can be said to consist of two elements, where each element is either an atom or a list. To trace through an arbitrary list requires an indefinite amount of storage to keep track of how to get back. The recursion mechanism provides this simply and succinctly. D. W. Barron's *Recursive Techniques in Programming* gives a lucid description of how to use recursion to advantage, and when to avoid it.

Use recursive procedures for
recursively-defined data structures.

We have presented a handful of tools for organizing computer programs. We have also shown what can happen if not enough care is taken in laying out the structure of a program. This is not to say that an intelligible program can be written only with the control structures we have presented. Nor can we guarantee that using just these tools will yield a readable program. But it helps.

The specific points of this chapter are:

(1) Data structure can make or break a program. Spend time on it.

(2) Write your program first in a made-up high-level language that you like, where you can see and debug your algorithm. When it is correct, translate it into whatever language you have a compiler for.

(3) The control-flow constructions in your virtual language should include:

The ability to group statements, as in PL/I's DO...END or BEGIN...END.

IF—THEN—ELSE, where the ELSE is optional.

CASE, which is a multi-way IF. In PL/I it can be written by augmenting an IF—THEN with a series of ELSE—IFs. In Fortran, the computed GOTO can sometimes serve.

DO—WHILE, which repeats a set of statements zero or more times while some condition is true. Note that the range of a Fortran DO is executed at least once, so the DO statement must be preceded by an IF whenever a zero or negative repeat count might occur.

BREAK and LOOP, which provide, respectively, an immediate exit from a DO—WHILE or a CASE, and a branch to the condition test of the DO—WHILE.

CALL, which modularizes your code into subroutines.

Your translation should be based on these constructions. GOTOs and labels are suspect; use them sparingly. Any GOTOs and labels in the final product should reflect these constructions only.

POINTS TO PONDER

3.1 In the quadratic equation solver, we kept the special code for the case where only C was zero. But the standard computation would produce

```
-B/(2.0*A) - SQRT(ABS(B**2))/(2.0*A)
```

which simplifies algebraically to −B/A, and

```
-B/(2.0*A) + SQRT(ABS(B**2))/(2.0*A)
```

which simplifies to 0.0. Does the computational result match the algebraic? Why do you think this case merits special handling?

3.2 The function

```
INTEGER FUNCTION TEST(BOARD,I,J)
INTEGER BOARD(8,8)
TEST = -1
IF (I.LT.1 .OR. I.GT.8 .OR. J.LT.1 .OR. J.GT.8) RETURN
IF (BOARD(I,J).GE.0 .AND. BOARD(I,J).LE.4) TEST = BOARD(I,J)
RETURN
END
```

returns a negative value if BOARD(I,J) is undefined or illegal; otherwise it returns BOARD(I,J). Rewrite subroutine STORE of the checker-playing program to use TEST. Add code to SEARCH to include valid single jumping moves. At most eight statements should have to be added. (Don't forget to add TEST to the INTEGER statement and increase the sizes of ROW and COL.)

What would be involved in adding jumps to the original version?

3.3 What simplifications can be made in the checker-playing subroutines if we use a 10 by 10 checkerboard, where the border squares contain negative values?

3.4 Rewrite our version of procedure DATES, using just one table of cumulative days:

```
DECLARE NDAYS(0:12) INITIAL(
    0,31,59,90,120,151,181,212,243,273,304,334,365);
```

Rewrite it using one non-cumulative table of days ("Let the machine do the dirty work."):

```
DECLARE NDAYS(0:12) INITIAL(
    0,31,28,31,30,31,30,31,31,30,31,30,31);
```

How do these approaches compare with the one we showed?

3.5 What happens to the original maze program if the top border looks like

```
...010...
...000...
.........
```

What if the top left corner looks like

```
110......
000......
.........
```

The POINT array can handle up to 60 loops. Can you define a maze that
has more than 60 loops? Remember that

```
...............
111111111111111
010101010101010
000000000000000
```

looks like seven loops when searched from left to right.

Does our version handle these cases correctly?

IV. INPUT AND OUTPUT

From June, 1972 *Computerworld:*

Slip of the Keypuncher's Finger Means
City to Lose $290,000 in Tax Revenue

WOONSOCKET, R.I. — A keypunch error compounded by a lack of programming safeguards will cost this city almost $300,000 in tax revenues this year.

The error occurred several weeks ago when the city's tax evaluation was being computed. It caused a 1967 Ford to be valued at over $7 million — $7,000,950 to be exact — and therefore cause the tax rate to be based on a figure that was about $7 million too high.

As a result, tax revenues will be decreased by $290,000, reported A. Robert Mailloux, finance director. The city will not increase the tax rate, so department heads will have to "pull in the belt," Mailloux said.

The error resulted when operators were preparing a test run for the property tax rolls on the municipal card-fed Honeywell 110. A keypunch operator mistakenly punched a "P" in the first column of a seven-column field.

The first four columns should have been empty, indicating that the automobile was only worth $950.

The logic of the computer, Mailloux related, stripped the zone bit from the field during a multiplication operation. The letter was thereby translated into a "7" and the next three blanks were filled with zeroes by the computer.

$182 Million Correct

The result, then, was $7,000,950 instead of $950 for the automobile; the total tax assessment for the city was originally reported as $187 million, based on an 80 rate, instead of the correct $182 million, Mailloux confirmed.

Tax revenues will be proportionately reduced, he added.

There were five checkpoints at which the erroneous card should have been detected and destroyed, he continued. In fact, the error was detected, and a new card punched, but the old card was not removed from the deck, despite the fact that a supervisor reported that it had been removed and destroyed.

Mailloux said the program should have contained checks that would not have permitted so great an assessment on an automobile to be processed.

59

A preparatory run by account number (taxpayer number) and another preparatory run by automobile registration number both should have detected the duplicate card, he related.

There were, however, "no programming safeguards," he stated. "Given human frailties, the program was the ultimate chance" to detect and avoid the error, he added.

The error was discovered two weeks ago, when the tax bills were mailed and the owner of the Ford received a bill for $290,000. Officials would not identify the recipient.

The error marks the "largest financial error in the city's history," according to local sources. Other observers suggested the $290,000 sum represented the largest amount ever lost, without compensation or recovery, for a computer-related error.

The actual loss will be increased if the city has to borrow money between now and the end of the fiscal year.

In twenty-five words or less, this article says that the assessment program did all its computations without checking that its input data made sense. There is a lesson here that every programmer must learn, usually the hard way (how would you like to be the programmer who wrote the assessment program?) and often several times: NEVER TRUST ANY DATA. Input prepared by people or even by other programs will contain errors. A good program tests its input for validity and, in critical cases like tax computations, for plausibility. (An automobile assessed at seven million dollars is not plausible.)

Many introductory programming texts contain variants of this problem:

Write a program to read three numbers A, B, and C, representing the sides of a triangle, and compute the area of the triangle.

Here is one solution:

```
      READ (5, 23) A, B, C
   23 FORMAT (3F10.0)
      S = (A + B + C) / 2.0
      AREA = SQRT(S * (S − A) * (S − B) * (S − C))
      WRITE (6, 17) A, B, C, AREA
   17 FORMAT (1P4E16.7)
      STOP
      END
```

In most ways this is a good program: it is well-formatted, and copies its input data to the output for visual inspection. The output format is well chosen: it uses the E format to handle very large or very small answers without losing significant digits, and the scale factor 1P to print one position before the decimal point, so the answers are in the form most familiar to readers. Our only minor complaint concerns the apparently random statement numbers.

But what happens if we test the program on the "triangle" (3, 1, 1)? Most probable is an unexpected termination with a diagnostic like "negative argument in SQRT," certainly an indirect way to report that the input does not represent a triangle. (And try it on $-1, -1, -1$.)

You should always "launder" your input: after S has been computed, verify that no side is too big (or negative). One programmer used PL/I's built-in function ANY to test each element of an array T which contains the lengths of the three sides:

```
        S = SUM(T)/2;
    IF ANY(T <=0)|ANY(T>S) THEN   it's not a triangle... ;

    IF ANY(T=S) THEN   it's a straight line... ;
    ...
```

The test for a straight line may not always be reliable, for reasons we shall explore in Chapter 5, but the generally suspicious approach is commendable. This checking is easy in PL/I. In Fortran, the same tests require more code, which may explain why they are not often made.

Test input for plausibility and validity.

Simple tests save later grief. Does the program read a parameter to define an array size? Then test that it does not exceed the array bounds. Here is part of a sort program:

```
        DIMENSION X(300)
C       READ NUMBERS TO BE SORTED.
        READ 1,N,(X(I),I=1,N)
      1 FORMAT(I3/(F5.1))
C       INITIALIZE TO MAKE N-1 COMPARISONS ON FIRST PASS.
        K=N-1
C       INITIALIZE TO BEGIN COMPARISONS WITH THE FIRST 2 NUMBERS.
      6 J=1
C       L IS USED TO RECORD THE FACT THAT AN INTERCHANGE OCCURS.
     19 L=0
C       MAKE COMPARISONS.
        DO 2 I=J,K
        IF(X(I)-X(I+1)) 2,2,3
      3 ...
```

There are minor flaws, such as the random statement numbers (again) and the use of an arithmetic IF where a logical IF would be more readable, but we will defer discussion of the full text until Chapter 6. For now, let us concentrate on the input statement.

Suppose N exceeds 300. Parts of storage outside the array X may be overwritten. Whatever happens after that will not be good, nor will it tell the user unequivocally what he did wrong. The program may even run to completion, but if the user does not look carefully at his output, he may not even notice that his program failed.

Some compilers (WATFOR, WATFIV, PL/I with SUBSCRIPTRANGE enabled, for instance) allow a check during execution that subscripts do not exceed array dimensions. This is a help, but not sufficient. First, many programmers do not use such compilers because "They're not efficient." (Presumably, this means that it is vital to get the wrong answers quickly.) Second, subscript range checking will not detect the other deficiency in this code. Suppose that the value of N is one. Then the program compares X(1) with X(2), which is not defined and probably garbage. If the garbage happens to be less than X(1), X(1) is gone forever, since it is sorted out of its position.

If we write a precise description of the *exact* input data for which the sort program works, we find, of course, that it fails for N outside the range 2 to 300. At that point, we might be embarrassed into making it do something sensible for all values of N:

```
      DIMENSION X(300)
      READ 10, N
   10 FORMAT(I3)
      IF (N.LT.1 .OR. N.GT.300) ... take error action ...
      READ 20, (X(I), I=1,N)
   20 FORMAT(F5.0)
      IF (N.EQ.1) ... leave routine, since in order ...
      ...
```

It may be easier to redo a program than to describe *exactly* what cases it works for. In any case, writing the description should point to bugs, and to areas for improvement. (The author of this sort program came close — his second and third comments both suggest that there might not be two items.)

Make sure input doesn't violate the limits of the program.

The statement

```
      READ 1,N,(X(I),I=1,N)
```

in the sort program illustrates a risky way to read data. N has to be computed by the user, probably by hand. Since people make mistakes, this is an error-prone operation, especially if N is at all large. And while the statement is compact, it does not leave room for the checking that is so important with this form of input. It should be avoided.

As we said before, computers count better than people; let them do the work. Mark the end of the data, then read until the marker is encountered. (In some languages, the marker can be implicit, as in the

```
ON ENDFILE ... ;
```

statement of PL/I or the END=... construction in some Fortrans.) You would be annoyed if you had to count correctly the number of cards in your source programs; thus compilers read until they find an END card. Do the same for *your* users.

Terminate input by end-of-file or marker, not by count.

The program below reads cards containing a name and a hair color, and totals the number of people with each color of hair.

```
      INTEGER NAME,COLOR,LAST,COL(6),COUNT(6)
      DATA COL/3HBLA,3HBLU,3HBRO,3HGRE,3HRED,3HWHI/,
     1 LAST,COUNT/4H0000,6*0/
    1 READ(5,2)NAME,COLOR
    2 FORMAT(A4,15X,A3)
      DO 3 I = 1,6
    3 IF( COLOR.EQ.COL(I) ) COUNT(I) = COUNT(I) + 1
      IF(NAME .NE. LAST) GO TO 1
      WRITE(6,4)
    4 FORMAT(12H COLOR COUNT)
      DO 5 I = 1,6
    5 WRITE(6,6)COL(I),COUNT(I)
    6 FORMAT(4X,A3,2X,I3)
      STOP
      END
```

Instead of forcing a user to count his data cards correctly, the program uses an explicit "end-of-file" test — a card with a name field of "0000" marks the end of the input. Excellent! But notice that the end-of-file test is made only *after* the data from the end-of-file marker card has been checked and accumulated. Should a color be punched in the "unused" field of the end-of-file card, it will corrupt the counts. This code may not fail often, but it is careless.

The use of mnemonics like "RED" and "BLU" instead of numeric codes like "1" and "2" is commendable, for it makes the program easier to use correctly. But if a color does not match any of the list, it is quietly skipped. Debugging input data is as important as debugging a program — some provision for locating bad input should always be included. In this case, each bad color should be printed (with an indication of which card is in error, for the deck may contain hundreds of cards.)

The program "works", but with negligible effort it can be improved:

```
      INTEGER NAME, COLOR, LAST, COL(6), COUNT(6), TOTAL
      DATA COL(1),COL(2),COL(3)/'BLA','BLU','BRO'/
      DATA COL(4),COL(5),COL(6)/'GRE','RED','WHI'/
      DATA LAST/'0000'/
      DO 10 I = 1,6
         COUNT(I) = 0
   10 CONTINUE
      TOTAL = 0
   20 READ(5,21) NAME, COLOR
   21 FORMAT(A4, 15X, A3)
      IF (NAME.EQ.LAST) GOTO 40
         TOTAL = TOTAL+1
         DO 30 I = 1,6
            IF (COLOR.NE.COL(I)) GOTO 30
               COUNT(I) = COUNT(I)+1
               GOTO 20
   30    CONTINUE
C                        FALL OUT IF BAD COLOR
         WRITE(6,31) COLOR, TOTAL
   31    FORMAT(' BAD COLOR - ', A3, ' IN CARD NUMBER', I5)
         GOTO 20
C                        END OF DATA INPUT
   40 WRITE(6,41) (COL(I), COUNT(I), I = 1,6)
   41 FORMAT(4X, A3, I5)
      STOP
      END
```

We have rendered the input loop as a large DO—WHILE (while the NAME is not equal to LAST). If a color is recognized, we count it and skip to the next case (GOTO 20 is a LOOP statement); otherwise we list the bad input color and then loop.

Identify bad input; recover if possible.

The same error, treating the end-of-file marker as legitimate data, is carried a step further in this program for computing student averages:

```
...
I=1;
/* INITIALIZE SUM */
IN: SUM=0;
/* READ SCORES AND COMPUTE SUM */
DO J=1 BY 1 TO 5;
GET LIST (SCORE(I,J));
SUM=SUM+SCORE(I,J);
END;
/* STOP READING IF FIRST SCORE IS NEGATIVE */
IF SCORE(I,1)<0 THEN GO TO OUT;
/* COMPUTE AVERAGE */
AVG(I)=SUM/5;
/* READ NAME */
GET LIST (NAME(I));
I=I+1;
/* GET NEXT STUDENT'S SCORES */
GO TO IN;
/* COMPUTE TOTAL NUMBER OF STUDENTS */
OUT: I=I-1;
/* PRINT ... */
...
```

The comments imply that scores and names are read until the first score is negative; this indicates the end of data. Unfortunately, what comments imply is not always precisely what happens. Because GET LIST reads free-form input, this program requires *five dummy scores* to terminate the DO loop that reads scores, although only the first need be negative. If less than five are given, the program encounters the end of the input unexpectedly, before the GET LIST is satisfied. Since no ENDFILE action has been specified, the program simply terminates without printing the desired output. This is not implied by the comments.

PL/I's explicit test for end-of-file is much superior to the Fortran-like mechanism used here. Let us use it to correct the error.

```
ON ENDFILE GOTO OUT;

DO I = 1 BY 1 TO IMAX;   /* LOOP UNTIL EOF OR ARRAYS FULL */
    GET LIST (SCORE(I,*), NAME(I));
        ... should check data for validity here ...
    AVG(I) = SUM(SCORE(I,*))/5;
END;
    ... get here if arrays are full ...

OUT:
    ... output processing ...
```

(A "*" subscript repeats an operation over all legal values of that subscript. Thus GET LIST (SCORE(I,*)) reads SCORE(I,1), SCORE(I,2), etc.; SUM(SCORE(I,*)) adds them all up.) We have dispensed with the negative dummy score for terminating the input. As an added bonus, we can easily avoid reading more input than the arrays can hold, by limiting the range of the DO loop that replaces

```
I=1;
IN:
   ...
I=I+1;
GO TO IN;
```

The ENDFILE condition provides an early BREAK from this loop. Then if we fall out of the loop, we know there is too much data for the program to handle. We also used a GOTO in the ON ENDFILE statement, rather than placing the output code there itself, so we could keep the code laid out in the order in which it is obeyed.

Explicit tests for end of file and the identification of faulty data make programs easier for people to use. So does input that is easy to prepare correctly:

From October, 1971 *Computerworld,*

Loss of One Digit Brings School Scheduling Snafu

KINGSTON, MASS. — One lost column in a punched card caused several high school classes to be scheduled for one room, while scores of other students wandered aimlessly all day long, for lack of a destination.

That's the description given by local and wire service reports of a computerized scheduling snafu at Silver Lake Regional High School here, but employees of the school "didn't know we had a big problem until we read about it in the paper."

There actually were some problems, originally blamed on keypunch errors, but they were not as severe as reported.

Assistant Superintendant Norman Donegan claimed the school committee was "not particularly upset" at the problems, which were reportedly settled in two or three days.

The matter has not been dropped, but there is no intense investigation either. Donegan indicated that the company involved in the error may lose the computer contract, which is worth $2000 a year, but that "we don't plan to stop scheduling by computer.

"In fact, we've even thought about increasing" the applications, he stated.

Donegan said that the error apparently was caused when the first digit in a three column field was dropped. The field indicates Teacher-Department-Subject, and with the omission of the teacher, the other categories became jumbled.

In other instances, the teacher indicated had left the school system, causing scheduling problems for students if a replacement had not been hired.

Leaving aside any question of why the program failed to check its input, this "minor" problem might never have happened if input formats were better suited to humans, and if mnemonics were used. Mnemonics make it easier for people to remember legal input and understand output, and they make it less likely that a keypunch error will transform one legal code into another one.

Here is a part of a program which computes prices of metals of various types and weights:

```
        ...
        KOUNT = 0
1       READ 6,WEIGHT,XMETAL
6       FORMAT(F10.1,3X,F4.1)
        KOUNT = KOUNT+1
        DATA BRAC1/0./,BRAC2/1000./,BRAC3/2000./,BRAC4/3000./,BRAC5/4000./
        DATA ALUM/1./,TIN/2./,COPPER/3./,BORON/4./
        IF(WEIGHT.LE.BRAC1)GO TO 100
        IF(WEIGHT.LT.BRAC2.AND.XMETAL.EQ.ALUM)GO TO 101
        IF(WEIGHT.LT.BRAC3.AND.XMETAL.EQ.ALUM)GO TO 102
        ...
        IF(WEIGHT.LT.BRAC3.AND.XMETAL.EQ.BORON)GO TO 118
        IF(WEIGHT.LT.BRAC4.AND.XMETAL.EQ.BORON)GO TO 119
        IF(WEIGHT.GE.BRAC5.AND.XMETAL.EQ.BORON)GO TO 120
        METAL=XMETAL
100     PRINT 200,WEIGHT,METAL,KOUNT
200     FORMAT(1X,9HWEIGHT = ,F10.1,8HMETAL = ,I2,27HERROR FOUND IN CARD N
       1UMBER I3)
        GO TO 1
101     COST=WEIGHT*3.00
        GO TO 300
102     COST=WEIGHT*2.75
        GO TO 300
        ...
118     COST=WEIGHT*1.50
        GO TO 300
119     COST=WEIGHT*1.25
        GO TO 300
120     COST=WEIGHT*1.00
300     METAL=XMETAL
        PRINT 301,KOUNT,METAL,WEIGHT,COST
301     FORMAT(1X,13HSHIPMENT NO.(,I2,1H),3X,7HMETAL= ,I2,3X,9HWEIGHT = ,F
       110.1,3X,7HCOST = ,F10.2)
        GO TO 1
```

The input data cards each contain a weight and a numeric code for a metal. There are twenty IFs in all to determine the weight bracket and metal to use for computation, and twenty different computations (statement numbers 101 through 120). Clearly, it would be better to put the prices in an array, indexed by metal type and weight class, and in fact the textbook from which the example was taken later gives a version of the program that does just that.

There are some other minor things to criticize. For instance, it is error-prone and inflexible to use a source card right up to the last column, as in statements 200 and 301. For example, FORMAT 200 leaves no space between the metal code and the word "ERROR". To fix this buglet, we must change both statement 200 and its continuation, then we must correct the character count (27) as well. If instead the card broke to a continuation at the end of a field, this problem would not arise, and only one change would be needed to fix the error:

```
200 FORMAT(1X, 'WEIGHT = ', F10.1, '  METAL = ', I2,
   $    '  ERROR FOUND IN CARD NUMBER ', I3)
```

The program has good points, too. It counts its data cards, instead of relying on the user. It copies the input onto the output (after computation) so it can be inspected visually. And, most important, it validates its input, testing for negative or zero weight and invalid metal code. It prints the offending card and its sequence number, then continues to the next data.

But our enthusiasm is tempered by discovering that if a negative or zero weight is encountered, the program prints the value of METAL for the *previous* input card. Label 100 is placed incorrectly, one statement too late.

If the conversion

```
METAL = XMETAL
```

were done once, immediately after the READ, the bug would vanish, and so would the need for statement 300 and the one before statement 100.

The other, more general, failing is the use of numeric codes (floating point at that) to name the metals. (Was floating point used because all the metals had names that were "floating point" variables in Fortran? What if we added LEAD, NICKEL, and IRON?) A typical line of output looks like

```
SHIPMENT NO.( 1)   METAL= 1   WEIGHT =    1000.0   COST =    2750.00
```

It is only after scanning the listing that we can deduce that metal 1 is aluminum.

The use of numeric codes is bad practice in a program which interfaces with people. The codes in this program are not even in alphabetical order. How can a user remember them? (As we mentioned, the textbook presents another version of this program a few pages later, which uses alphabetic names instead of numeric codes for the metals, but discards all error checking.)

Make input easy to prepare and output self-explanatory.

Here is an example that shows ill-chosen mnemonics:

Write a program segment that will assign sales area 1 to each even salesman, and sales area 2 to each odd salesman.

```
      DIMENSION SALESM(17)
      DO 20 IJ=1,17
10    IF(IJ/2*2-IJ) 12,11,12
11    SALESM(IJ)=1.
      GO TO 20
12    SALESM(IJ)=2.
20    CONTINUE
```

The curious expression IJ/2*2−IJ is a Fortran idiom that determines whether IJ is evenly divisible by two. The original problem can be solved more clearly and succinctly with the MOD function:

```
      DIMENSION SALESM(17)
      DO 20 I = 1,17
         SALESM(I) = MOD(I,2)+1
   20 CONTINUE
```

We are more concerned here with the mnemonic values chosen: even-numbered salesmen have an odd number, while odd-numbered salesmen have an even number. This is backwards. It is certainly no more difficult to let "1" be the code for odd-numbered salesmen, and "2" the code for even. (We leave it to the reader to decide whether using a floating point array to hold integer values is an appropriate data structure.)

Programs should not only cope with incorrect input, but also encourage users to make fewer errors by being easy to use. Consider this input fragment:

```
      READ(1,4) XIHP(I),R(I),FORCE(I),NREV(I)
    4 FORMAT(F5.1,F3.1,F3.0,I2)
```

If you are an occasional user of this program, will you be able to remember, a week from now, that the XIHP field is five columns wide, R and FORCE are three, and NREV is two? Not likely. There would be less to remember if the author had used a uniform format, like

```
4 FORMAT(3F5.0, I5)
```

in which all fields have the same width. This also leaves room for future growth — whatever NREV is, it may someday be bigger than 99, which is all the I2 format permits. I2 is not only non-uniform, but restrictive.

You might even consider doing this:

```
      READ(1,4) XIHP(I), R(I), FORCE(I), REV
    4 FORMAT(4F5.0)
      NREV(I) = REV
```

Now we do not need to right-justify the integer NREV — we enter it with a decimal point like everything else, and convert it internally. (As it turns out, the only place in the program where NREV is used is in a long product where all the other factors are floating point. So it might as well have been declared floating point anyway.)

Use uniform input formats.

The difference between F3.1 and F3.0, by the way, lies in the interpretation of an input number that does not contain a decimal point. If the number contains a decimal point, as it should for reliability, the explicit point overrides the decimal point position in the FORMAT statement. Floating point input specifications should thus be restricted to the form Fn.0. (We have quietly made this change in most of our examples so far.) Omitting decimal points to make fields smaller is penny-wise, pound-foolish.

While we are making uniform formats, consider this excerpt from a program in another text:

```
      READ (5,100) MAX,JLOW,JHIGH
  100 FORMAT (I3,2I4)
      ...
      READ (5,7) N(I)
    7 FORMAT (I4)
      ...
```

Here two (randomly numbered) FORMAT statements are used, because the pointless irregularity in the first means that it cannot be used with the second READ. (Did the programmer use I3 because he "knew" that MAX would never exceed 999? Users now have to learn two formats; when the program grows, they may have to learn a third.) Do it this way:

```
      READ(5, 100) MAX, JLOW, JHIGH
100 FORMAT(315)
      ...
      READ(5,100) N(I)
```

The idea is not to save the small space represented by a second FORMAT, but to make life simpler for the user. Even if you prefer to write FORMATs after each I/O statement (a good practice), make them as similar as possible.

Formats should also be chosen with some thought to the probable device used to create input — usually a keypunch or a terminal. Free-form input is easiest; next best are uniform fields near the left end of the card or line. Imagine typing with this format, even after the missing comma is inserted:

```
      GET EDIT(X,ZILCH)(X(10),F(4)X(65),A(1));
```

If possible, numbers should be justified left, not right. (That was the purpose of our floating-to-fixed conversion above.) Spread the data out a little — cramming it into the absolute minimum space makes it too hard for reading by people, who may well have to look at it to find errors.

Make input easy to proofread.

The ideal arrangement for reading numbers, especially for getting programs working quickly, is free-form input, where the data layout is essentially unspecified.

Free-form input is easy in PL/I:

```
      GET LIST (A, B, C);
```

reads input until it finds three numbers. These can be on one card or line, or on several, separated by blanks or commas.

Not all Fortran implementations allow free-form input, but some, especially for interactive systems, do provide unrestricted input, often as

```
      READ A, B, C
```

You must weigh the question of portability against ease of use right here and now. In this case, our vote goes to ease of use.

Use free-form input when possible.

Here is a READ statement that gets five variables:

```
   READ(1,10) KONST1,KONST2,FEED,DIAM,RPM
10 FORMAT(I6,I6,F5.3,F5.3,F4.0)
```

Suppose you had to use this program periodically (after negotiating to have the input format made more uniform). Without looking, is the third argument the feed rate or the diameter? If you last used the program a week ago, would you remember? When there are many (i.e., more than one or two) arguments or parameters to be provided to a program, let the user specify his parameters by name; that way he has to input only what he wants changed from the default, and he doesn't have to remember any particular order.

Parameters can be read directly by name with the GET DATA statement of PL/I. Input like

```
   FEED=27.0    DIAM=3.5    RPM=3600.0
```

lets the user give input arguments in an arbitrary order and format, as long as he can remember what the names are. Fortran's NAMELIST feature does the same thing, although it is nonstandard and its use is clumsy.

If input parameters are supplied by name, you can use default values in a graceful way. If some parameter is normally given a certain value, build that value into the program; then if the user does not specify its value, he will get the built-in value "by default." (Of course the defaults have to be chosen intelligently, to satisfy some significant fraction of the user population.) And print out the defaulted values as well as the inputs, so the user will know what the program did.

Use self-identifying input. Allow defaults.
Echo both on output.

Input/output is the interface between a program and its environment. Two rules govern all I/O programming: NEVER TRUST ANY DATA, and REMEMBER THE USER. This requires that a program be as foolproof as is reasonably possible, so it behaves intelligently even when used incorrectly, and that it be easy to use correctly. Ask yourself: Will it defend itself against the stupidity and ignorance of its users (including myself)? Would I want to have to use it myself?

To summarize the major principles discussed in this chapter:

(1) Check input data for validity and plausibility.

(2) Make sure that data does not violate limitations of the program.

("Garbage in, garbage out" is not a law of nature, but a commentary on how well principles (1) and (2) are followed in practice.)

(3) Read input until end-of-file or marker, not by count.

(4) Identify input errors and recover if possible. Do not stop on the first error. Do not simply ignore errors.

(5) Use mnemonic input and output. Make input easy to prepare (and easy to prepare correctly). Echo the input and any defaults onto the output; make output self-explanatory.

POINTS TO PONDER

4.1 Suppose someone were to ask you to write a program to process question-
naires and print summaries. There are twenty questions per form, which
he offers to have punched in ten eight-column fields per card, using the
code:

> 0 — disagree
> 1 — agree
> 2 — don't care

Assuming that the person who has to do the keypunching is a friend of
yours, what changes would you suggest in the input format? What changes
would make your programming job easier?

4.2 Fortran ignores most blanks in program statements, but treats most blanks
as zeros in input data. Thus

```
    READ(5,10) N
 10 FORMAT(I5)
    IF (N .EQ. 1 024) WRITE(6,20) N
 20 FORMAT(1X, I5)
```

will cause the input number

> 1 024

to be stored as 10024 by the READ statement, but compared to 1024 in the
IF.

Can you think of any benefit to be gained from this inconsistency? How
can you avoid any trouble it might cause?

4.3 One text states that Fortran is unable to neatly output a rectangular array
whose dimensions are computed at run time. That is, it would be nice to
be able to write

```
    DIMENSION A(10,10)
    ...
    NROWS=...
    NCOLS=...
    ...
    WRITE(3,101) ((A(I,J),J=1,NCOLS), I = 1,NROWS)
101 FORMAT (NCOLS(3X,F8.2)/)
```

but in Fortran it is illegal to use a variable in a FORMAT statement.

To avoid this problem, the text advocates reading a FORMAT specification at run time, together with the alphabetic values of the numbers up to NCOLS, and using them to patch up the FORMAT:

```
       DIMENSION A(10,10),NFMT(10),NUM(10)
       READ (1,101) NUM,NFMT
  101  FORMAT(10A4/10A4)
       ...
       NROWS=...
       NCOLS=...
       ...
       NFMT(2) = NUM(NCOLS)
       WRITE(3,NFMT) ((A(I,J),J=1,NCOLS),I=1,NROWS)
Input
    1   2   3   4   5   6   7   8   9  10
 (         (3X,F8.2)/)
```

Discuss the merits of this maneuver, in terms of cleanliness, potential for user error, and portability between various computers. You might wish to contrast it with the following solution:

```
       DO 110 I = 1,NROWS
          WRITE(3,101) (A(I,J), J=1,NCOLS)
  101     FORMAT ('0', 10(F11.2))
  110 CONTINUE
```

4.4 Write a free-form input subroutine that works from a pre-specified array of variable names. How much more work is required to allow for defaults? Once you have such a subroutine, how much harder is it to input variables of different types (say INTEGER as well as REAL variables)? How much harder is it to input elements of an array?

V. COMMON BLUNDERS

A major concern of I/O programming is making sure that a program works correctly when given bad input data. But even having correct data is no guarantee that a program will work. In this chapter we will discuss other aspects of making software reliable.

We begin, appropriately enough, with initialization, for failing to set a variable to some value before using it is a fruitful source of error. For example:

```
        DOUBLE PRECISION FUNCTION SIN(X,E)
  C     THIS DECLARATION COMPUTES SIN(X)TO ACCURACY E
        DOUBLE PRECISION E,TERM,SUM
        REAL X
        TERM=X
        DO 20 I=3,100,2
        TERM=TERM*X**2/(I*(I-1))
        IF(TERM.LT.E)GO TO 30
        SUM=SUM+(-1**(I/2))*TERM
     20 CONTINUE
     30 SIN=SUM
        RETURN
        END
```

This program is a straightforward implementation of the Maclaurin series for SIN(X):

$$SIN(X) = X - X**3/3! + X**5/5! - ...$$

Although large values of X will cause truncation errors long before convergence, it will work for small values of X.

At least it should, if properly programmed. But what is the value of SUM when it is first referenced inside the loop? A search shows that SUM has never been set to anything, so it begins as garbage and in most systems accumulates more garbage with each successive call. This oversight is readily corrected, *if it is detected.* How do we find it? We might run some sample cases and compare them with a table or with another sine routine. (The latter is better because it is faster and less prone to error.) The important thing, however, is to check, for a casual look at the output may not always reveal that something is amiss.

77

Make sure all variables are initialized before use.

It would be well to test this routine further, for it is still incorrect. Suppose X is negative upon entry, as it may often be. Then TERM is negative, and remains so after it is recomputed just inside the DO loop. So it will be less than E, and an immediate exit will take place. The "sine" computed, needless to say, is worthless. We replace the test by

```
IF (DABS(TERM).LT.E) GOTO 30
```

and now we have a working sine routine.

Or do we?

Where there are two bugs, there is likely to be a third. Look at the clever expression used to provide alternating signs for successive terms:

```
(-1**(I/2))
```

Is this expression "minus one to an integer power," as desired, or "one to an integer power, with a minus sign in front," which is always minus one? We encountered a similar expression in Chapter 2 that happened to work right. This one happens to work wrong.

Additional parentheses should be used in either case to remove all ambiguity. Even better, the computation inside the DO loop should be rewritten as

```
TERM = -TERM*X**2/FLOAT(I*(I-1))
SUM = SUM + TERM
IF (DABS(TERM).LT.E) GOTO 30
```

and the whole issue is avoided. Notice that we increment SUM *before* testing TERM, so the last term computed is added in before we exit. This corrects the *fourth* bug in the routine. (Exercise: determine if we *now* have a working sine routine.)

Don't stop at one bug.

Sometimes there are several initialization errors, as in this code:

```
C       CURRENT COMPUTING PROGRAM
C       INPUT VALUES FOR RESISTANCE,FREQUENCY AND INDUCTANCE
        READ(5,20) R,F,L
    20 FORMAT(3F10.4)
C       PRINT VALUES OF RESISTANCE,FREQUENCY AND INDUCTANCE
        WRITE(6,30) R,F,L
    30 FORMAT(3H1R=,F14.4,4H  F=,F14.4,4H  L=,F14.4)
C       INPUT STARTING AND TERMINATING VALUES OF CAPACITANCE,AND INCREMENT
        READ(5,40) SC,TC,CI
    40 FORMAT(3F10.6)
C       SET CAPACITANCE TO STARTING VALUE
        C=SC
C       SET VOLTAGE TO STARTING VALUE
        V=1.0
C       PRINT VALUE OF VOLTAGE
    50 WRITE(6,60) V
    60 FORMAT(3H0V=,F5.0)
C       COMPUTE CURRENT AI
    70 AI = E / SQRT(R**2 + (6.2832*F*L - 1.0/(6.2832*F*C))**2)
C       PRINT VALUES OF CAPACITANCE AND CURRENT
        WRITE(6,80) C,AI
    80 FORMAT(3H0C=,F7.5,4H  I=,F7.5)
C       INCREASE VALUE OF CAPACITANCE
        C = C + CI
        IF (C .LE. TC) GO TO 70
C       INCREASE VALUE OF VOLTAGE
        V = V + 1.0
C       STOP IF VOLTAGE IS GREATER THAN 3.0
        IF (V .LE. 3.0) GO TO 50
        STOP
        END
```

This program is thoroughly, even excessively, commented. Most of the input parameters are printed out for inspection and verification. But there are several errors that warrant discussion. To begin with, what is the value of E when statement 70 is executed? Again we must search through the code to find that it has never been set.

On some computer systems, storage is initialized to zero at the beginning of a run; in such cases, this bug should come to light when it is observed that the current is zero for all values of C and V. But if storage is left at some random value, which is true on many systems, the current computed will be wrong (although it might look plausible).

Simple oversight is the most common way to botch initialization. However, it seems likely that this particular error arose because the programmer was not clear in his mind whether voltage was V (a mnemonic) or E (common usage among electrical engineers, to whom this problem is directed).

There are other troubles with this program. Since L is not declared REAL, it is an integer by default. What happens when an integer variable is read in and printed out with a floating point (F) format? We do not know for certain, but we can guess that it will not likely be what was wanted. The missing declaration for L also means that statement 70 contains a mixed-mode expression. If the version of Fortran in use accepts mixed mode, the line will be executed, but probably incorrectly, because it will use whatever has been placed in L as if it were an integer.

Most serious is the error in logic. The program prints the values of C and AI for a series of capacitances, while V is 1.0. Then when C exceeds TC, V is increased by 1.0 (to 2.0), and we return to statement 50. But C is never reinitialized to SC, so after printing *one* value of AI with V equal to 2.0, we immediately increment V to 3.0. We then print one more value of AI (again with C beyond TC), and stop.

It is improbable that this is what the program should do. C has not been initialized to SC each time that V is changed. Whenever you have to build a loop out of spare parts because a DO statement is not suitable, take pains to display clearly how the control parameters are initialized, incremented and tested:

```
C                                   LOOP ON V
      V = 1.0
   50    WRITE(6,60) V
   60    FORMAT('0', 'VOLTAGE=', F5.0)
C                                   LOOP ON C
         C = SC
   70       AI = V/SQRT(R**2 + (6.2832*F*L - 1.0/(6.2832*F*C))**2)
            WRITE(6,71) C, AI
   71       FORMAT('0', 'CAPACITANCE=', E16.5, '  CURRENT=', E16.5)
            C = C + CI
            IF (C .LE. TC) GOTO 70
         V = V + 1.0
         IF (V .LE. 3.0) GOTO 50
      STOP
      END
```

We will have more to say later in this chapter about the questionable wisdom of using a floating point increment like

```
      C = C + CI
```

to step through a set of values, but for the moment we will let it pass.

A more subtle failure to initialize occurs in this example:

```
      DIMENSION NUM(80),NALPHA(80)
      DATA NBLANK /1H /
      READ (5,101) NALPHA,NUM
  101 FORMAT (80A1,T1,80I1)
      NUM = 0
      N = 0
      DO 30 I = 1,80
      IF (NALPHA(I) .EQ. NBLANK) GO TO 30
      N = N + 1
      NSUM = NSUM + NUM(I)
   30 CONTINUE
```

The problem here is that, although the statement

```
NUM = 0
```

is illegal (NUM after all is an array), many Fortran compilers will treat this as

```
NUM(1) = 0
```

a throwback to Fortran II, where it was legal. The effect is to conceal the typographical error that made NSUM into NUM, wipe out NUM(1) unintentionally, and leave NSUM uninitialized. What will happen? That will be a surprise for the program's users. (In PL/I the offending statement would set *all* of the array NUM to zero. This would make the error quite visible.) Use variable names that are not too similar, so typos will stand out.

Finding initialization errors is difficult and time-consuming. If you have access to a compiler that checks whether variables have been set before being used (such as WATFOR, WATFIV, or PL/C), use it. Worrying about the "cost" of using a debugging compiler is false economy. Your time is worth more than the small amount of machine time involved. More to the point, you may not find out about some error until it is too late.

Use debugging compilers.

There is another type of faulty initialization which will not be detected by debugging compilers. It occurs regularly in code which uses Fortran's DATA statement to set values. Here is an excerpt from a program we have already seen in Chapter 4:

```
INTEGER NAME,COLOR,LAST,COL(6),COUNT(6)
DATA COL/3HBLA,3HBLU,3HBRO,3HGRE,3HRED,3HWHI/,
1 LAST,COUNT/4H0000,6*0/
...
```

Suppose this free-standing program is converted to a subroutine. If the programmer forgets to replace the DATA statement that initializes COUNT by executable code like

```
DO 10 I = 1,6
   COUNT(I) = 0
10 CONTINUE
```

the subroutine will fail when called a second time, because the old values will remain in COUNT. The rule is: use DATA for things that are truly constant, like the table of colors in the example; execute initializing code for variables, like counts and sums.

In PL/I, the INITIAL attribute re-initializes AUTOMATIC variables upon each invocation of a procedure, so the problem is less severe. But you should still distinguish between true constants and initialized variables; declare them separately, and comment them clearly.

Initialize constants with DATA statements or INITIAL attributes;
initialize variables with executable code.

Another familiar class of errors is called "off-by-one": some action is done once too often, or one time too few, because a test is botched or an index is wrong. Let us look at some examples. Here is part of a program for processing customer accounts:

```
    CTR = 0;
  GO TO OVFLO;
  RDCARD: READ FILE (CARDIN) INTO (CARD);
/*TABLE LOOKUP FOR VALID CUSTOMER NUMBER*/
    LOOP: DO I = 1 TO 20;
      IF CARD.NUM = NUM_TBL(I)
    THEN GO TO NN;
            ELSE;
      END;
    GO TO RDCARD;
    NN: ...

  IF CARD.AMT > 0 THEN GO TO CR_RTN;
            ELSE GO TO DR_RTN;
    CR_RTN: DETAIL.CREDIT = CARD.AMT;
    DETAIL.DEBIT = 0;
      WRITE FILE (PRTFLE) FROM (DETAIL);
            GO TO TST_CTR;
    DR_RTN: DETAIL.DEBIT = CARD.AMT;
    DETAIL.CREDIT = 0;
      WRITE FILE (PRTFLE) FROM (DETAIL);
    TST_CTR: CTR = CTR + 1;
            IF CTR > 45 THEN GO TO OVFLO;
            ELSE GO TO RDCARD;
    OVFLO:
  WRITE FILE (PRTFLE) FROM (HDR);
  WRITE FILE (PRTFLE)   FROM (COL_HDR);
  WRITE FILE (PRTFLE) FROM (LINE);
    CTR = 0;
  GO TO RDCARD;
```

Let us deal with the bug first. What happens if there are exactly 46 transactions, or 92, or any multiple of 46? Sure enough, the column headings are printed on an extra page, even though there is no data to go under them. The test for end-of-page should be before line 47 is printed, not after line 46.

While we are fixing the error, we can improve the program a great deal. We can add error handling, if desired, rather than ignoring invalid data. We can also use relational operators and compound statements to eliminate the labels and GOTOs, the extra WRITE statement, and the redundant ELSE clause of line 8. And we can format the code to better emphasize the program structure.

```
CTR = 46;
DO WHILE ('1'B);
   READ FILE (CARDIN) INTO (CARD);

/* LOOK FOR VALID CUSTOMER NUMBER */
   IF ¬ANY(NUM_TBL = CARD.NUM) THEN
      WRITE FILE (ERROR) FROM (CARD);
   ELSE
      DO;   /* NORMAL PROCESSING */
         IF CARD.AMT>0 THEN
            DO;
               DETAIL.CREDIT = CARD.AMT;  DETAIL.DEBIT = 0;
            END;
         ELSE
            DO;
               DETAIL.DEBIT = CARD.AMT;  DETAIL.CREDIT = 0;
            END;

         IF CTR >= 46 THEN  /* HEADER ON NEW PAGE */
            DO;
               WRITE FILE (PRTFLE) FROM (HDR);
               WRITE FILE (PRTFLE) FROM (COL_HDR);
               WRITE FILE (PRTFLE) FROM (LINE);
               CTR = 0;
            END;

         WRITE FILE (PRTFLE) FROM (DETAIL);
         CTR = CTR + 1;
      END;
END;
```

The failure to use relational operators and DO groups is a weakness common to Fortran programmers recently converted to PL/I. As we saw in Chapters 2 and 3, you should use the features of the language that make correct coding easier.

Watch out for off-by-one errors.

A common cause of off-by-one errors is botching a test, for example by using "greater than" when "greater than or equal to" is actually needed. The program from which the following code is taken finds the smallest of a set of numbers. The text says that "Any number equal to or greater than the contents of LOWI is by-passed by a transfer of control to the CONTINUE statement." Here is the code:

```
      LOWI = LOW(1)
      DO 12 I=2,N
      IF(LOWI-LOW(I)) 12,13,13
13    LOWI = LOW(I)
12    CONTINUE
```

LOWI is *not* set to the first minimum value, as the text implies, but to the last, because equality causes LOWI to be updated. A near miss indeed; fortunately it makes no real difference in this trivial situation. One hopes to be equally lucky in bigger programs. (This example illustrates once again how opaque the Fortran arithmetic IF can be; avoid it.)

The code examines an undefined element (LOW(2)) if N is one, a circumstance that is quite possible in a general purpose routine. But it will work correctly, if the least bit more slowly, if the DO limit is made one instead of two. When we do this, we can also clarify the rest of the code:

```
      LOWI = LOW(1)
      DO 12 I = 1,N
         IF (LOW(I).LT.LOWI) LOWI = LOW(I)
12    CONTINUE
```

Take care to branch the right way on equality.

Here is an instance where branching the wrong way on equality results in a real, though small, error. The code computes a table of monthly balances and interest charges for a given principal amount, interest rate, and monthly payment.

```
DECLARE (A,R,M,B,C,P)    FIXED DECIMAL (13,4);

L10:GET LIST (A,R,M);
    PUT EDIT ('THE AMOUNT IS',A)(A(13),F(10,2))
             ('    THE INTEREST RATE IS',R)(A(23),F(6,21))
             ('    THE MONTHLY PAYMENT IS',M)(A(25),F(8,2));
    IF M<=A*R/1200 THEN GO TO L30;
    PUT SKIP(3)EDIT
('          MONTH       BALANCE    CHARGE        PAID ON PRINCIPAL')(A);
    PUT SKIP;
    B=A;
DO I=1 TO 60;
  C=B*R/1200;
  IF B+C<M THEN GO TO L20;
  P=M-C;   B=B-P;
  PUT SKIP EDIT (I,B,C,P)(F(13),3 F(13,2));
END;
L20:PUT SKIP(2)EDIT ('THERE WILL BE A LAST PAYMENT OF:',B+C)
                                        (A(35),F(8,2));
    GO TO L10;
L30:PUT SKIP(2)EDIT ('UNACCEPTABLE MONTHLY PAYMENT')(A);
    GO TO L10;
```

What happens if the amounts are such that the balance due plus the interest charge (B+C) just happens to equal the monthly payment M (within one-half cent)? The program takes an extra trip around the loop, recomputes B and C, and informs the user that "THERE WILL BE A LAST PAYMENT OF: 0.00". This is graceless.

We can patch the code to read

```
IF B+C<0.005 THEN GO TO L10; /* FINAL PAYMENT ALREADY MADE */
IF B+C<M THEN GO TO L20;
```

but it would be better to reorganize it completely, so that it reads from top to bottom instead of branching about.

There is also an instance here of a familiar error. Notice that there are two exits from the DO loop, one from the side and one from the bottom, that arrive at the same place. This should always arouse suspicion. The program is designed to exit normally from the side (with a BREAK) when the loan is paid off with sixty payments or fewer, and from the bottom when it is not. What happens if it does exit from the bottom? The final payment is B+C, but although B has been recomputed to be the correct remaining balance, C is not recomputed before being used — it is the interest charge left over from the previous payment. Clearly the interest charge should be either zero, or recomputed from the new B, depending on whether the final payment is made immediately or after another month.

In either case, this is an error. (It must be coincidental that it is in the bank's favor.) Our version avoids this problem with the safer DO—WHILE construction. As we repair the code we can correct the illegal F(6,21) format item in the first PUT statement, and add a SKIP so the headings are placed on a new line instead of being tacked onto the end of whatever message was printed previously.

```
DECLARE (A, R, M, C, P) FIXED DECIMAL(13,4);

TOP:
   GET LIST (A, R, M);
   PUT SKIP(3) EDIT ('THE AMOUNT IS', A) (A, F(10,2))
       ('   THE INTEREST RATE IS', R) (A, F(6,2))
       ('   THE MONTHLY PAYMENT IS', M) (A, F(8,2));
   C = A*R/1200;
   IF C>=M THEN
      DO;
          PUT SKIP(2) EDIT ('UNACCEPTABLE MONTHLY PAYMENT') (A);
          GOTO TOP;
      END;
   PUT SKIP(3) EDIT
       ('MONTH', 'BALANCE', 'CHARGE', 'PAID ON PRINCIPAL')
       (X(8), A, X(6), A, X(7), A, X(3), A);
   PUT SKIP;
   DO I = 1 TO 60 WHILE (A+C>=M);
      P = M - C;
      A = A - P;
      PUT SKIP EDIT (I, A, C, P) (F(13), 3 F(13,2));
      C = A*R/1200;
   END;
   IF A+C>=0.005 THEN
      PUT SKIP(2) EDIT ('THERE WILL BE A LAST PAYMENT OF:', A+C)
          (A, X(5), F(10,2));
   GOTO TOP;
```

The interest charge C is now up-to-date whenever it might be referenced. Note that we could have avoided even the one label we used, by making the program into an explicit DO—WHILE and putting the calculation into an ELSE clause, as we did in the customer-account example above. The choice is a matter of taste. We did, however, eliminate the unnecessary variable B, since extraneous variables are always undesirable.

Be careful when a loop exits to the same place
from side and bottom.

Here is another example of a common error. The program is a binary search procedure to find out where in a table X an element A lies. If the table contains an entry that matches A, both of the indices LOW and IHIGH should point to that value; otherwise LOW and IHIGH should be the indices of the two table elements immediately below and above the input value A. The elements of the array X are already sorted into increasing order.

```
      DIMENSION X(200),Y(200)
      READ 50, N
50 FORMAT(I5)
 2 READ 51, (X(K), Y(K), K = 1, N)
51 FORMAT (2F10.5)
      READ 52,A
52 FORMAT (F10.5)
      IF (X(1)-A)41, 41, 11
41 IF(A-X(N))5, 5, 11
11 PRINT 53,A
53 FORMAT(1H ,F10.5,
 1       26H IS NOT IN RANGE OF TABLE.)
      STOP
 5 LOW = 1
      IHIGH = N
 6 IF (IHIGH-LOW-1)7, 12, 7
12 PRINT 54, XLOW, YLOW, A, XHIGH, YHIGH
54 FORMAT(1H 5F10.5)
      STOP
 7 MID = (LOW + IHIGH)/2
      IF (A-X(MID))9, 9, 10
 9 IHIGH = MID
      GO TO 6
10 LOW = MID
      GO TO 6
      END
```

First we correct statement 12 to refer to the arrays X and Y, with the appropriate subscripts X(LOW), X(IHIGH), and so on. Presumably this error arose from a careless transcription from mathematical notation to Fortran. The program does not check that N is in range, but it does test whether A is inside the table range, which is good.

What happens if we try to search a table containing only one entry? LOW and IHIGH are both set to one, so we immediately go to statement 7, which sets MID to one as well. Now, since A equals X(1) (A has been tested to be sure it is in the table), we branch to statement 9, where IHIGH is set to one (which does not change it!) and we return to statement 6. LOW and IHIGH are still both set to one, so we immediately go to statement 7.... This program will run for a long time.

The problem is that not all possible reasons for terminating the search loop were taken into account. We could patch the code simply by testing whether N is one and providing special handling, but before we do, let us examine another case. Suppose that the table contains several entries, and that the entry at X(1) happens to match A. Then IHIGH and MID will steadily converge toward 1, while LOW remains at 1. When IHIGH gets to either 3 or 4, MID is set to 2;

then since A is less than X(2), IHIGH is set to 2. Now IHIGH—LOW is 1, so the IF at statement 6 sends us to statement 12, and we exit. LOW and IHIGH are left pointing at X(1) and X(2) even though there is an exact match at X(1). We leave it to the reader to decide how pervasive this error is.

Patching is no substitute for rewriting:

```
      DIMENSION X(200), Y(200)
      READ 21, N
   21 FORMAT(I5)
      IF (1.LE.N .AND. N.LE.200) GOTO 30
         PRINT 23, N
   23    FORMAT(' BAD INPUT COUNT:', I10)
         STOP
   30 READ 31, (X(I), Y(I), I=1,N)
   31 FORMAT(2F10.5)
      READ 31, A
      IF (X(1).LE.A .AND. A.LE.X(N)) GOTO 40
         PRINT 33, A, X(1), X(N)
   33    FORMAT(' ', F10.5, ' IS OUT OF TABLE RANGE', 2F10.5)
         STOP
   40 LOW = 1
      IHIGH = N
   50 IF (IHIGH—LOW .LE. 1) GOTO 60
         MID = (IHIGH+LOW)/2
         IF (A.LE.X(MID)) IHIGH = MID
         IF (A.GE.X(MID)) LOW = MID
         GOTO 50
   60 IF (A.EQ.X(LOW)) IHIGH = LOW
      IF (A.EQ.X(IHIGH)) LOW = IHIGH
      PRINT 61, X(LOW), Y(LOW), A, X(IHIGH), Y(IHIGH)
   61 FORMAT(' ', 5F10.5)
      STOP
      END
```

Our search loop is a DO—WHILE (while IHIGH—LOW>1) that can, under some circumstances, be performed *zero* times. Degenerate cases frequently arise where a piece of code has nothing to do — in this instance, when N is one or two, no search is necessary. In such cases it is important to "do nothing" gracefully; the DO—WHILE has this useful property.

Fortran programmers who make DO—WHILEs with DO loops should remember that the Fortran DO loop is *always* done once, regardless of its limits; an explicit test is necessary to "do" it zero times.

Make sure your code "does nothing" gracefully.

How can a conscientious programmer avoid errors like those we have shown? How can he test his code to eliminate those that do creep in? The last few examples have illustrated what might be called "boundary-condition" errors, errors that arise at a critical data value or decision region. Things go wrong only there, not for the vast majority of cases "in the middle."

So it seems likely that one good strategy, both for writing and for testing, is to concentrate on the boundaries inherent in the program. For example, in the binary search above, we might guess that since the search is based on powers of two, reasonable places to look for bugs are at values of N of 2^k, 2^k-1, and 2^k+1, Of course one boundary is always the trivial or null case, here when N equals one. And we hit the jackpot.

But we should have learned by now to be suspicious: where one bug is found, there may be an infestation. So we looked at another boundary, the case where the table contained a match for the input entry. And again we hit the jackpot.

Test programs at their boundary values.

The text-centering program of Chapter 3 contained an error that caused a reference outside the bounds of an array. We found that bug by testing with data that completely filled the array, clearly a boundary condition. Sometimes, however, a storage over-writing error is so flagrant that it can be caught without even that much testing, as in this code that groups school grades by tens:

```
      DO 40 I = 1,N
C
C        TEST IF DATA IS IN RANGE
C
      IF(MARKS(I) .LT. 1 .OR. MARKS(I) .GT. 100) GO TO 30
C
C        TRANSFORMATION TO DIRECTLY DETERMINE CLASS INTERVAL MEMBERSHIP
C
      J = MARKS(I) - 1/10 + 1
      NCLASS(J) = NCLASS(J) + 1
      GO TO 40
   30 WRITE(3,102)MARKS(I)
  102 FORMAT(' ***MKS001 - DATA OUT OF RANGE ', I12)
   40 CONTINUE
      ...
```

Let us look at that transformation

```
      J = MARKS(I) - 1/10 + 1
```

What is the 1/10 for? We know that 1/10 is zero in Fortran, since integer division truncates. This means that J is always set to MARKS(I)+1, so the program will write far beyond the bounds of NCLASS (which is dimensioned to hold 10 values). Evidently some parentheses are missing; the code should read

```
J = (MARKS(I)-1)/10 + 1
```

We might also note that the program checks the data for validity (why is a mark of zero invalid?), but does not tell us where in the data the offending entries lie. Why not say

```
  30 WRITE(3,102) I, MARKS(I)
 102 FORMAT(' SERIAL NUMBER', I5, ' MARK', I10, ' OUT OF RANGE')
```

Another test procedure to keep in mind is simply to hand-compute a few answers and compare them with the machine solution. The following code computes, among other things, the mean and the variance of a set of observations. The mean is the sum of the observations, divided by the number; the variance is the difference between the sum of squares and the average squared sum, all divided by one less than the number of observations. (Got that?) Now look at the code:

```
C       COMPUTE MEAN
        XBAR = SUMX / AN
C       COMPUTE VARIANCE
        VAR = (SUMSQ - (SUMX**2 / AN)) / AN - 1.0
```

The author has included a flowchart that states, correctly, that the variance is defined to be

```
(...)/(number of observations-1)
```

and AN is clearly the number of observations, as a floating point number. But the code leaves out the parentheses. This is an error, but not an obvious one if the user is in the habit of believing everything that comes out of a computer. Do a few cases yourself; then when the answers do not agree, find out why. (The discrepancy between code and flowchart illustrates one of the problems of documentation. See Chapter 7 for more.)

_____

Check some answers by hand.

_____

Floating point variables add a new spectrum of errors, all based on the fact that the machine can represent numbers only to a finite precision. Here is a simple example, a program which integrates a polynomial between two limits, by a trapezoidal approximation:

```
      AREA=0.
      X = 1.
      DELTX=0.1
9     Y=X**2+2.*X+3.
      X=X+DELTX
      YPLUS=X**2+2.*X+3.
10    AREA=AREA+(YPLUS+Y)/2.*DELTX
      IF(X-10.)9,15,15
15    WRITE(2,7)AREA
7     FORMAT(E20.8)
      STOP
      END
```

This should evaluate the function for X=1.0, 1.1, ..., until X is 10.0, should it not? But try it, and you will discover that on many machines it in fact does an extra evaluation, the last one at X=10.09999.... The reason is simple: "0.1" is not an exact fraction in a binary machine (in much the same way that 1/3 is not an exact fraction in a decimal world); its nearest representation in most machines happens to be slightly less than 0.1. Thus 10 times "0.1" is not 1.0000..., but is 0.9999..., and by extension, when "0.1" is added to 1.0 ninety times, the result is not 10.000..., but 9.999.... The test that terminates the loop is sensitive to the difference, and gives us an extra trip around.

The value of the integral is too high by over two percent for this function and range. This error could have been readily caught, since the function can be integrated by hand. The discrepancy might then have led to further analysis of the program. (People who worry about computing efficiency might also notice that the function is evaluated twice as often as it need be. Since the answers are wrong, however, this seems unimportant.)

The moral? Floating point numbers should never be used for counting. If you want intervals of 0.1, do it this way:

```
      AREA = 0.0
      X = 1.0
      Y = X**2 + 2.0*X + 3.0
      DELTX = 0.1
C                   STEPS OF 0.1 FROM 1.1 TO 10.0
      DO 10 I = 11,100
         X = FLOAT(I)/10.
         YPLUS = X**2 + 2.0*X + 3.0
         AREA = AREA + DELTX*(YPLUS+Y)/2.0
         Y = YPLUS
10    CONTINUE
```

continued on next page

```
   WRITE(2,20) AREA
20 FORMAT(1PE20.8)
   STOP
   END
```

This also eliminates the redundant function evaluations.

10.0 times 0.1 is hardly ever 1.0.

As a spectacular example of what floating point errors can lead to, when compounded at a million instructions per second, let us look at these two programs, from consecutive pages of a text, each of which produces a table of natural logarithms:

```
Program 1:
  PUT EDIT ((LOG(A) DO A=1 TO 9.99 BY .01))(F(10,6));
```

```
Program 2:
  DECLARE A FIXED DECIMAL (4,2);

  DO A=1 TO 9.9 BY .1;
    PUT EDIT (A)(F(5,2));
    PUT EDIT ((LOG(A+B) DO B=0 TO .09 BY .01))(X(5),10 F(9,5));
  END;
```

We would hope that these produce identical tables, save for formatting. Since the text reproduces some of the output of these programs, let us show the values obtained for the logarithms of 3.00, 3.01, 3.02, 3.03:

```
Program 1:
  1.098563  1.101891  1.105208  1.108513  ...
```

```
Program 2:
  1.09861   1.10193   1.10525   1.10856  ...
```

A third of the way through the table, these differ by five parts in a hundred thousand, an uncomfortable error. Why are the answers so different? As a wise programmer once said, "Floating point numbers are like sandpiles: every time you move one, you lose a little sand and you pick up a little dirt." And after a few computations, things can get pretty dirty.

One of the first lessons learned about floating point numbers is that tests for exact equality between two computed floating point numbers are almost certain to fail. For example,

```
C       RIGHT TRIANGLES
        LOGICAL RIGHT, DATA
        DO 1 K = 1,100
        READ (2,10) A, B, C
C       CHECK FOR NEGATIVE OR ZERO DATA
        DATA = A.GT.0. .AND. B.GT.0. .AND. C.GT.0.
        IF(.NOT.DATA) GO TO 2
C       CHECK FOR RIGHT-TRIANGLE CONDITION
        A = A**2
        B = B**2
        C = C**2
        RIGHT = A.EQ.B+C .OR. B.EQ.A+C .OR. C.EQ.A+B
1       WRITE(3,11) K, RIGHT
        CALL EXIT
C     ERROR MESSAGE
2       WRITE(1,12)
        STOP
10      FORMAT(3F10.4)
11      FORMAT(I6,L12)
12      FORMAT(11H DATA ERROR)
        END
```

The checking of input data is a step in the right direction, but not as comprehensive as we would like; and we prefer somewhat more intelligible output. But the test for right triangles will fail on virtually all fractional values, because of truncation errors. For example, the triangle A=3.0, B=4.0, C=5.0 will be recognized as right-angled on almost all machines. But if we scale the values down by a factor of ten, the triangle A=0.3, B=0.4, C=0.5 will often not be "right-angled." The code has to be replaced by some criterion of "near enough." (And this must be relative, not absolute, as we saw in Chapter 1.)

Don't compare floating point numbers solely for equality.

We do not have space to go more deeply into the mysteries of floating point computation; that is the province of numerical analysts. We intend only to emphasize that floating point computations should be used cautiously when controlling an algorithm. They should seldom be used for counting, nor should two computed floating point values be compared only for equality.

Let us summarize the main lessons of this chapter. Remember that the errors that we have shown are by no means all that can happen; they represent the common ones.

(1) Initialize variables before using them. Be sure that variables in subroutines and inner loops are properly reset between successive uses. Set constants at compile time and variables at run time. If a debugging compiler is available to check for initialization errors, use it.

(2) Watch for off-by-one errors. Be sure that things are done the right number of times, and that comparison tests branch the right way on equality.

(3) Check that array references do not go out of bounds. Again, if subscript-range checking is available from your compiler, use it.

(4) When a DO loop is designed to exit from the side, write code to handle the case where it exits from the bottom.

(5) Test your program at its internal boundaries. This should be done before the program is run, and as a running check. Ask whether each loop might be performed zero times under some circumstances, and if you are writing in Fortran, augment DO statements with IFs if they may have to be skipped.

(6) Do not count with floating point numbers. Do not expect fractional floating point values to obey the familiar laws of arithmetic — they do not.

POINTS TO PONDER

5.1 An interesting number to know is EPS, the smallest floating point number such that

$$1.0 + EPS > 1.0$$

Write a subroutine to compute EPS for any reasonable class of machines. (Discussion of this and related parameters may be found in M.A. Malcolm, Algorithms to Reveal Properties of Floating Point Arithmetic, CACM 15, Nov. 1972.) How would you write convergence tests to make use of EPS?

5.2 This program computes the mean of a set of numbers. The end of the data is marked by a card containing a number greater than or equal to 99999. The program "works for any number of data items up to 5000."

```
100     FORMAT(5F15.5)
        SUM = 0.
        DO 3 N = 1,5000
        READ(2,100) X
        IF (X - 99999.)3,4,4
3       SUM = SUM + X
4       XNUM = N - 1
        XMEAN = SUM/XNUM
        WRITE(3,100)XMEAN
```

True or false? (Hint: Try a couple of boundary conditions.)

5.3 We observed that one should never test floating point numbers for exact equality. But here is one case where any rational person would believe that the comparison would work:

```
 95 N = N+1
    READ (5,100) DATA(N)
100 FORMAT(F10.3)
    IF(DATA(N).NE.999.999) GO TO 95
```

If the input card contains 999.999 in the proper field, the program will stop reading, will it not? Try this case and similar ones on your system.

On some systems, the routines in the compiler that convert "999.999" into its internal (binary) representation were written by different people than those who wrote the routines that convert "999.999" when a READ is executed. Why are the routines not identical, since they perform the same function? (Answer: That is the state of the art of computing, and one of the reasons for this book.)

5.4 Now that you are alert to the perils of testing floating point numbers for equality, try fixing

```
C      FIRST ATTEMPT FOR APPROXIMATING AREA UNDER A CURVE
    1 AREA=0.0
      READ(2,10)T
   10 FORMAT(F10.4)
      H=0.1
      X=0.0
    2 XN=-X
      AREA=AREA+(6.0*(2.0**XN)+6.0*(2.0**(XN-H)))*0.1/2.0
      X=X+H
      IF(X-T)2,8,9
    8 WRITE(3,33)AREA
   33 FORMAT('AREA =',F8.5)
      GO TO 1
    9 CALL EXIT
      END
```

Do you think just changing the IF to

```
IF (X-T) 2, 8, 8
```

is sufficient?

5.5 "Defensive programming" means anticipating problems in advance, and coding to avoid errors before they arise. What could you do to the following program fragments in the way of defensive programming?

(a) This is the entire body of a procedure for computing the arcsine of X in degrees:

```
IF X = 1 THEN RETURN(90);
ELSE RETURN(ATAND(X/SQRT(1-X**2)));
```

(b) This subroutine is supposed to rotate the rows of array B by one position (i.e. row 1 goes into row M, row 2 goes into row 1, ... and row M goes into row M−1). C is used as temporary storage.

```
      SUBROUTINE ROTATE (B, M, N, C)
      DIMENSION B (M, N), C (N)
      DO 24 I = 1, N
      C (I) = B (M, I)
      B (M, I) = B (1, I)
   24 CONTINUE
      MM = M - 2
      DO 34 I = 1, MM
      DO 34 J = 1, N
      B (I, J) = B (I + 1, J)
   34 CONTINUE
```

continued on next page

```
      DO 44 I = 1, N
      B (M - 1, I) = C (I)
44    CONTINUE
      RETURN
      END
```

Rewrite this code to rotate a column at a time instead of a row at a time. Which is easier?

VI. EFFICIENCY AND INSTRUMENTATION

Machines have become increasingly cheap compared to people; any discussion of computer efficiency that fails to take this into account is shortsighted. "Efficiency" involves the reduction of overall cost — not just machine time over the life of the program, but also time spent by the programmer and the users of the program.

A clean design is more easily modified as requirements change or as more is learned about what parts of the code consume significant amounts of execution time. A "clever" design that fails to work or to run fast enough can often be salvaged only at great cost. Efficiency does not have to be sacrificed in the interest of writing readable code — rather, writing readable code is often the only way to ensure efficient programs that are also easy to maintain and modify.

To begin, let us state the obvious. If a program is not correct, it matters little how fast it runs. For instance:

```
C       PAYROLL COMPUTATION PROGRAM
C       READ EMPLOYEES ID,HOURS WORKED AND PAY RATES
     10 READ(5,20) EMPID,HOURS,SRATE,ORATE
     20 FORMAT(2F5.0,2F5.2)
        IF(EMPID .EQ. 77777.0)GO TO 60
        IF(HOURS .GT. 40.0)GO TO 50
C       COMPUTE WEEKLY PAY
        WAGE = SRATE * HOURS
C       CONVERT EMPLOYEES ID TO FIXED POINT FOR PRINTOUT
        IEMPID = EMPID
C       PRINT EMPLOYEES ID AND WAGE
     30 WRITE(6,40) IEMPID,WAGE
     40 FORMAT(12H1EMPLOYEE ID,I5,7H   WAGE,F8.2)
        GO TO 10
C       COMPUTE OVERTIME PAY
     50 A = ORATE * (HOURS - 40.0)
C       COMPUTE BASE PAY
        B = SRATE * 40.0
C       COMPUTE TOTAL WAGE
        WAGE = A + B
        GO TO 30
     60 STOP
        END
```

After we unscramble the confusing flow of control, we can see that the integer version of the employee's ID, IEMPID, is not set correctly when there is overtime — its value is that left over from the last employee who had no overtime. The cause is trivial — IEMPID is not set immediately after input. A similar instance of this error appears in Chapter 4.

Disorganized code often leads to errors. One wonders if the excessively complicated structure of this program comes from an attempt to be "efficient." There are two distinct cases (overtime or not), with a different wage calculation for each. In order to test HOURS only once per employee, these cases are separated and then brought back together again incorrectly.

But if we test HOURS twice:

```
IF (HOURS .LE. 40.0) WAGE = SRATE * HOURS
IF (HOURS .GT. 40.0) WAGE = SRATE*40.0 + ORATE*(HOURS-40.0)
```

indeed we do an extra test. But the program is simpler: two lines replace six, the unnecessary variables A and B disappear, and the logic flows directly from beginning to end. Not only is it now correct, but it can be seen to be correct.

Splitting the computation into two parts, only one of which is done, is preferred if each half requires a complicated calculation. But the code should still flow from top to bottom:

```
        IF( HOURS .GT. 40.0 ) GOTO 25
        ... standard calculation ...
        GOTO 30
   25 ... overtime calculation ...
   30 WRITE ...
```

in the standard IF—THEN—ELSE fashion.

Make it right before you make it faster.

Another all-too-common situation where small-scale attempts to tweak code into being faster lead to a potential error is exemplified by this excerpt, which we have already seen in Chapter 5.

```
        LOWI = LOW(1)
        DO 12 I=2,N
        IF(LOWI-LOW(I)) 12,13,13
   13   LOWI = LOW(I)
   12   CONTINUE
```

A subroutine should be able to cope with reasonable and even unreasonable input. The simple expedient of changing the DO limits from 2,N to 1,N indeed adds an extra "wasted" comparison, but guarantees that the program will correctly find the minimum of a vector of one element, a task that the original version fails to perform. The more general version would look like:

```
      FUNCTION LOWEST(LOW, N)
      DIMENSION LOW(N)
      IF (N.LE.0) STOP
      LOWEST = LOW(1)
      DO 10 I = 1,N
          IF (LOW(I).LT.LOWEST) LOWEST = LOW(I)
   10 CONTINUE
      RETURN
      END
```

Make it fail-safe before you make it faster.

Here is another example, which replaces the first N elements of the array A with their factorials:

```
      SUBROUTINE ARRFAC (A,N)
      DIMENSION A(100)
      INTEGER A
      DO 2 I=1,N
      IF (A(I))2,2,4
C     FACTORIAL PROGRAM
    4 K=A(I)
      NFACT=1
      IF(K.EQ.1) GO TO 8
      DO 6 J=2,K
    6 NFACT=NFACT*J
    8 A(I)=NFACT
    2 CONTINUE
      RETURN
      END
```

Special handling is given the case where K (alias A(I)) equals one (but why doesn't the test branch to statement 2 instead of to 8?). Certainly the code runs slightly faster if K is one, but the program is more involved. Remove the test, change the inner DO limits to J=1,K, and the program still works well. Of course, it would be better if zero factorial were properly computed (it equals one), instead of being skipped as an error. Nor would it hurt to assign the statement numbers in increasing order.

Make it clear before you make it faster.

If the utmost in speed were of any importance here, the way to get it is obviously not to test whether K is one, but to pre-compute a table of factorials, and index into that directly. The table will not be bigger than 15 or 20 entries on any current computer, since the factorials rapidly get too large to store as exact integers. We have remarked several times that a change in data representation often simplifies control structure more profoundly than any amount of tweaking. Efficiency likewise depends strongly on how the data is structured.

This brings us to another important point: simplicity and clarity are often of more value than the microseconds possibly saved by clever coding. For instance, in the code below, one text suggests that

```
DO 4 J = 1,1000
4 X(J) = J
```

be replaced by

```
Z = 0.0
DO 4 J = 1,1000
Z = Z + 1.0
4 X(J) = Z
```

presumably to avoid a thousand conversions to floating point.

This is an excellent example of nit-picking. One compiler we tried compiled the first loop into nine machine instructions, the second loop into eight. If all instructions were to take about the same time, the time saving would be a little over ten per cent. If this loop is ten per cent of an entire program (which seems high, since it is clearly just an initialization), the "improved" program would run one percent faster. As a matter of fact, the "improved" code uses a higher proportion of floating point instructions, which are more time consuming, so any saving is debatable. A second compiler *increased* the number of instructions for the "improved" version from ten to eleven, making the program slower! Trivia rarely affect efficiency. Are all the machinations worth it, when their primary effect is to make the code less readable?

Don't sacrifice clarity for small gains in "efficiency."

Sometimes a preoccupation with minutiae lets obvious things slip by unnoticed. In the code

```
I = K + 1
DO 6 J = 1,30
6 A(J) = B(J) * C(I)
```

one text observes correctly that C(I) is a constant within the loop, and thus there is no need to make the subscript computation repeatedly. The suggested remedy is

```
I = K + 1
TEMP = C(I)
DO 6 J = 1,30
6 A(J) = B(J) * TEMP
```

Many compilers will do the trivial optimization of moving constants out of a loop without being asked. (By knowing too much, you may even impede their efforts.) But even for a simple compiler, the first two lines should certainly read

```
TEMP = C(K+1)
```

Let your compiler do the simple optimizations.

The attempt to re-use pieces of code often leads to tightly knotted programs, difficult to get right, to understand, and to modify later, as in this program that decides if a number is prime:

```
ST1: GET LIST(N);
   IF N¬>1 THEN
      PUT EDIT('ILLEGAL INPUT N=',N,' <= 1')(SKIP,X(10),A,F(5),A);
   ELSE DO; IF N<=3 THEN GO TO APRIME;
      IF N=2*FLOOR(N/2) THEN  NOPRIME: PUT EDIT(N,' IS NOT A PRIME ',
         'NUMBER')(SKIP,F(15),2 A);
      ELSE DO; DO R=3 TO SQRT(N) BY 2; IF N=R*FLOOR(N/R) THEN
         GO TO NOPRIME; END /* OF DO LOOP */;
APRIME: PUT EDIT(N,' IS A PRIME NUMBER')(SKIP,F(15),A); END; END;
   GO TO ST1;
```

The dilemma seems to have been how to avoid duplicating the PUT statement that reports non-primes. The resulting code is almost unreadable. (This is partly the fault of its layout, which we will comment on in Chapter 7.) For instance, it contains a transfer from within an ELSE to the beginning of the corresponding THEN! And instead of using the MOD function to test divisibility, it simulates Fortran's truncating division with the FLOOR function. The code cries out for reorganization:

```
ST1: GET LIST(N);
     IF N<=1 THEN
        DO;
           PUT EDIT ('ILLEGAL INPUT N=', N, ' <= 1')
              (SKIP, X(10), A, F(5), A);
           GOTO ST1;
        END;

     IF N>3 THEN
        DO R = 2, 3 TO SQRT(N) BY 2;   /* R = 2,3,5,7,... */
           IF MOD(N, R) = 0 THEN
              DO;
                 PUT EDIT (N, ' IS NOT A PRIME NUMBER')
                    (SKIP, F(15), A);
                 GOTO ST1;
              END;
        END;

  /* GET HERE FOR N=2 OR 3 OR IF FALL OUT OF LOOP */
     PUT EDIT (N, ' IS A PRIME NUMBER') (SKIP, F(15), A);
     GOTO ST1;
```

Although "longer" because it is better spaced, this version actually contains fewer statements. It is easy to read; the only GOTOs are used to implement LOOP statements, branching back to the input statement, which has the only label. (Both versions check the input for validity, which is commendable.)

Don't strain to re-use code; reorganize instead.

A faster-running program is often the by-product of clear, straightforward code. As an example, this program computes N! for N = 3,5,...,49.

```
C FACTORIAL PROGRAM
      DOUBLE PRECISION FACTOR, X
      NAMELIST /OUT/I,FACTOR
      DO 100 I =3,50,2
      FACTOR = I
      J =I-1
      DO 200 K=1,J
      X=K
  200 FACTOR = FACTOR*X
  100 WRITE (6,OUT)
      STOP
      END
```

Admittedly one does not compute a table of odd factorials very often, but this program is needlessly complicated and wasteful, because it recomputes N! from scratch for each N, instead of just multiplying the previous value by $N*(N-1)$. Here's the simpler version:

```
      DOUBLE PRECISION FACTOR, X
      NAMELIST /OUT/ I, FACTOR
      FACTOR = 1.0D0
      DO 100 I = 3,50,2
         FACTOR = FACTOR * FLOAT(I*(I-1))
         WRITE(6,OUT)
100   CONTINUE
      STOP
      END
```

Students of complexity theory will recognize that the first version requires computing time proportional to N^2; the second takes time proportional to N. The absolute amount of computer time saved in this specific case is obviously irrelevant, but the gain in intelligibility is significant.

The author of the factorial program, by the way, included some of the machine-generated answers from his program. The value of 3! is given as

```
      5.999999999999999
```

Other values, also integers, are printed just as badly. The I/O routines provided by this particular compiler (*not* by the text-book author) are a typical example of false economy (that is, misplaced efficiency), since they clearly do not produce the most meaningful answer for the user. Not only did the routine distort what was almost certainly an exact floating point 6.0 in its haste, but it then decided (presumably) that it was "too inefficient" to round the decimal representation before printing it.

As another example where a straightforward design leads to a simpler program, consider this excerpt from a program for finding the smallest and largest of a set of numbers:

```
      IF( A .GT. SMALL ) GO TO 2
      IF( A .LT. SMALL ) SMALL = A
      GO TO 3
 2    IF(A .GT. BIG ) BIG = A
 3    ...
```

This can be replaced by

```
      IF (A .LT. SMALL) SMALL = A
      IF (A .GT. BIG) BIG = A
```

and the code is just as fast, and probably smaller.

The Euclidean Algorithm computes the greatest common divisor of two integers KA and KB by a series of divisions. Here is part of a program to do it. (KA and KB are positive.)

```
      IF(KA—KB)  5, 5, 4
   4  KR = KA
      KA = KB
      KB = KR
   5  IF(KA)  6, 7, 6
   6  KR = KB — KB/KA*KA
      KB = KA
      KA = KR
      GO TO 5
   7  PRINT 102, KB
```

Mathematicians have grown used to assuming that KA is less than or equal to KB in the algorithm, and so when the program is implemented, the first four lines of code make sure this is the case. But a moment's reflection shows that if KA is greater than KB, the algorithm works anyway, since the first pass through the procedure does the reversal. Removing the explicit interchange shrinks the code by a factor of two, without increasing its complexity. At the same time we can use the MOD function to improve the readability:

```
   5  IF (KA.EQ.0) GOTO 7
      KR = MOD(KB,KA)
      KB = KA
      KA = KR
      GOTO 5
   7  ...
```

This is of course a DO—WHILE — the division is repeated while KA is not zero. And notice that it can be done zero times.

Make sure special cases are truly special.

Let us turn to sorting, an area where efficiency is important in practice. Here is an interchange sort:

```
      DIMENSION X(300)
C     READ NUMBERS TO BE SORTED.
      READ 1,N,(X(I),I=1,N)
    1 FORMAT(I3/(F5.1))
C     INITIALIZE TO MAKE N-1 COMPARISONS ON FIRST PASS.
      K=N-1
C     INITIALIZE TO BEGIN COMPARISONS WITH THE FIRST 2 NUMBERS.
    6 J=1
C     L IS USED TO RECORD THE FACT THAT AN INTERCHANGE OCCURS.
   19 L=0
C     MAKE COMPARISONS.
      DO 2 I=J,K
      IF(X(I)-X(I+1)) 2,2,3
C     AN INTERCHANGE IS TO TAKE PLACE.
C     IS THIS THE FIRST INTERCHANGE.
    3 IF(L) 20,21,20
C     RECORD POINT OF FIRST INTERCHANGE LESS ONE POSITION.
   21 J1=I-1
C     MAKE INTERCHANGE.
   20 SAVE=X(I)
      X(I)=X(I+1)
      X(I+1)=SAVE
C     RECORD POINT OF LAST INTERCHANGE (ACTUALLY ALL INTERCHANGES).
      L=I
    2 CONTINUE
C     DETERMINE IF NUMBERS ARE IN SEQUENCE.
      IF(L) 8,9,8
C     NUMBERS ARE NOT YET IN SEQUENCE.  SET DO PARAMETERS.
    8 K=L
C     DO NOT WANT TO START AT ZERO SO TEST J1 FOR VALUE OF 0.
      IF(J1) 6,6,7
    7 J=J1
      GO TO 19
    9 PRINT 16,N
      ... print numbers, etc.
```

In Chapter 4 we mentioned the perils of making the user specify the number of data points to be input rather than letting the machine do the counting. We have also discussed how this type of code fails when N is less than two. Similarly, we have often pointed out that arithmetic IF's are inadvisable, for they are less clear to the reader (Quickly! Does it sort up or down?), and always add the possibility of arithmetic over- or underflow. And the hodge-podge of statement numbers makes it unnecessarily difficult to find one's way around the code.

But our primary subject is "efficiency." Inspection reveals that this sort program is carefully coded to squeeze most of the possible speed out of the basic algorithm. A switch L determines whether the table has been sorted in less than the maximum N−1 passes, so an early exit can be taken. The index J increases to skip over elements known to be already in order at the beginning of the array. The upper index K decreases over those in order at the end. The programmer has carefully avoided the trap of letting J become zero. And there are plenty of comments to explain what is going on. All in all, this should be a marked improvement over a basic no-bells-and-whistles version.

Let us put that hypothesis to the test, by constructing another sort program and comparing run times on identical data. Here is the interchange sort, absolutely devoid of frills. We do not even bother to eliminate comparisons between an element and itself.

```
      SUBROUTINE SORT(X, N)
      DIMENSION X(N)
C              SORT INCREASING, BY INTERCHANGE
      IF (N.LT.2) RETURN
      DO 20 I = 2,N
         DO 10 J = 1,I
            IF (X(I).GE.X(J)) GOTO 10
               SAVE = X(I)
               X(I) = X(J)
               X(J) = SAVE
  10     CONTINUE
  20 CONTINUE
      RETURN
      END
```

This has about half as many lines of code as the "efficient" sort, and is simple enough that comments seem superfluous. We have coded it as a subroutine, a more likely usage. (Notice the immediate return if N is less than 2.)

How much faster is the "efficient" program than the simple-minded one? We eliminated the I/O statements from the former and made it into a subroutine, so we could directly compare sort times without I/O overhead. Then we sorted arrays of uniformly distributed random numbers (several arrays of each size). Here are some run times, in milliseconds:

size	"efficient"	simple	ratio
10	1	1	1.0
50	22	19	1.15
300	850	670	1.25
2000	38500	29200	1.3

As we might have anticipated, complexity again loses out to simplicity: not only has carefully-tailored code produced a 15 to 30 percent *increase* in run time, but the ratio appears to be getting worse as the size goes up.

Keep it simple to make it faster.

Although the simpler code is faster, it is still time-consuming for larger arrays — 30 seconds to sort 2000 numbers is extravagant *if it is done often.* (Done infrequently, it is probably irrelevant; the programmer time needed to make a noticeable improvement in speed is certainly more valuable than a few minutes of machine time.)

How can we really speed it up? Fundamental improvements in performance are most often made by algorithm changes, not by tuning. Let us demonstrate.

It is well known in the sorting business that the interchange sort is suitable only for sorting a handful of items. Here is a simple version of a procedure known as the Shell sort (after D. L. Shell). Conceptually it is similar to the "efficient" sort we began with, and certainly no more complicated.

```
      SUBROUTINE SHELL(X, N)
      DIMENSION X(N)
C  SORTS UP.  IF THERE ARE NO EXCHANGES (IEX=0) ON A SWEEP
C  THE COMPARISON GAP (IGAP) IS HALVED FOR THE NEXT SWEEP
      IGAP = N
    5 IF (IGAP.LE.1) RETURN
      IGAP = IGAP/2
      IMAX = N-IGAP
   10    IEX = 0
         DO 20 I = 1,IMAX
            IPLUSG = I+IGAP
            IF (X(I).LE.X(IPLUSG)) GOTO 20
               SAVE = X(I)
               X(I) = X(IPLUSG)
               X(IPLUSG) = SAVE
               IEX = IEX+1
   20    CONTINUE
         IF (IEX.GT.0) GOTO 10
      GOTO 5
      END
```

Here are the run time comparisons, in milliseconds:

size	"efficient"	simple	Shell
10	1	1	1.7
50	22	19	20
300	850	670	260
2000	38500	29200	3200

The run times speak for themselves — not only is the Shell sort faster by a factor of nine at 2000 elements, but the rate of increase is lower. (Be it noted that the Shell sort is *not* the fastest sort available; it is merely an easy step up from the usual interchange sorts.)

There are two lessons. First, time spent selecting a good algorithm is likely to pay larger dividends than time spent polishing an implementation of a poor method. Second, for any given algorithm, polishing is not likely to significantly improve a fundamentally sound, clean implementation. It may even make things worse.

Don't diddle code to make it faster — find a better algorithm.

Our conclusions about the sort programs are based on measurements, not on *a priori* notions of what will or will not be efficient. For example, theoretical studies predict that for large values of N, the Shell sort will be substantially faster than any interchange sort, for its run time grows as no more than $N^{1.5}$ instead of N^2. Common sense says that for small N, interchange sorts will be faster because they are simpler.

Neither theory nor common sense tells us where the cross-over takes place; that depends on programming. Measurements show that, for our particular programs, the transition takes place for N around 50, but that the disparity is not impractical even at N=300.

These measurements are obtained by using a timing package to time a particular piece of code, like this:

```
CALL TICK(TIME)
... code to be timed ...
CALL TICK(TIME)
```

TIME is set to the elapsed computation time since the last call to TICK, to whatever resolution the operating system provides. Most computer systems provide such a service. (An even better service, less commonly available, times each subroutine without any need to explicitly reference the timing package in the program being timed.)

Timing is not always sufficient. For example, precisely why is the simple sort faster than the "efficient" one? The real work of each is in comparisons and exchanges; the rest is bookkeeping. Could it be that the simple sort is faster because somehow it does much less real work, or does it just do less bookkeeping?

Instrumenting the program to make a simple measurement gives us the clue. We add two counters, NCOMP and NEXCH, to each program:

```
      ...
C               COUNT COMPARISONS
      NCOMP = NCOMP+1
      IF (X(I).GE.X(J)) GOTO 10
C               OUT OF ORDER; EXCHANGE AND COUNT
      NEXCH = NEXCH+1
      SAVE = X(I)
      ...
```

The counters are initialized and printed outside the sort. Here are the results (including the Shell sort):

size	"efficient"	simple	Shell	
10	43	54	60	comparisons
	22	22	13	exchanges
50	1020	1280	880	
	570	570	150	
300	41000	45100	11500	
	22400	22400	1500	
2000	1920000	2000000	147000	
	1000000	1000000	18600	

The two interchange sorts do the same number of exchanges. But, although the "efficient" sort does fewer comparisons than the simple sort, the saving does not offset the cost of all the other operations. With some confidence we can conclude that the simple sort is faster because its bookkeeping is simpler. (The Shell sort column shows conclusively why it is faster than the others for large N.)

Beware of preconceptions about where a program spends its time. This avoids the error of looking in the wrong place for improvements. Of course, you have to have some working idea of which part of a program has the most effect on overall speed, but changes designed to improve efficiency should be based on solid measurement, not intuition.

A useful and cheap way to measure how a program spends its time is to count how many times each statement is executed. The resulting set of counts is called the program's "profile" (a term first used by D. E. Knuth in an article in *Software Practice and Experience,* April, 1971). Some enlightened computer centers make available a "profiler" to do this automatically for your program. (It works by temporarily adding "N=N+1" statements to relevant parts of the program.)

Instrumentation such as counts, profiles, and subroutine timings helps you concentrate effort on those parts of the code which really need improvement. Although we have already obtained improvements without the aid of the profiler, we can illustrate its potential. Here is a program that collates grades, counting right and wrong answers for each student:

```
      ISUM=0
      DO 3 I=1,5
      IF(CORANS(I).EQ.STUANS(I))GO TO 4
      ICHECK(I)=0
      GO TO 30
    4 ICHECK(I)=1
      ISUM=ISUM+1
   30 IWRONG=5-ISUM
    3 CONTINUE
```

If we take the profile of this code, we observe that the statement

```
   30 IWRONG=5-ISUM
```

is executed five times for each student. Why is this necessary? Clearly the number of wrong answers need only be computed once, after we know how many were right (assuming there are no other possibilities).

The code contains a "performance bug" — although correct, it does more work than necessary, because of redundant code. The statement should be outside the loop, with its label removed and the GO TO 30 changed to GOTO 3.

Instrument your programs.
Measure before making "efficiency" changes.

The cost of computing hardware has steadily decreased; software cost has steadily increased. "Efficiency" should concentrate on reducing the expensive parts of computing.

Let us summarize the main points of this chapter.

(1) If a program is wrong, it doesn't matter how fast it is. Get it right before you start to "improve" it.

(2) Keep code clean and straightforward — don't try to make it fast while coding.

(3) Don't worry about optimizing every little calculation. Trying to outsmart a compiler defeats the purpose of using one.

(4) Worry about the algorithm, not about the details of code. Remember that data structure can profoundly affect how an algorithm must be implemented.

(5) Instrument a program during construction. Measure before deciding on "efficiency" changes. Leave the instrumentation in as the program evolves.

POINTS TO PONDER

6.1 In our local computer center, control cards must be in a fixed format: there must be a dollar-sign in column 1, the operation (e.g., "FORTRAN") begins in column 8, and any additional information begins in column 16. Any deviation in any card typically causes the run to be aborted. Less than 30,000 control cards are submitted per day.

(a) If processing free-form input were to add 100 microseconds per card of operating system overhead (a generous allowance), what would this flexibility cost per day? (Answer: 3 seconds.)

(b) What does it cost one user to have to re-submit one job because of a mispunched card?

(c) Debate the pros and cons of free- versus fixed-format input from the users' and the system's viewpoints.

(d) Find some analogous examples of short-sighted economy at your computer center.

(e) [Term project] Try to get them changed.

6.2 Statement-frequency counts (profiles), although useful measurement tools in a simple language like Fortran, break down to some extent in more complex languages like PL/I, where a single "statement" can involve substantial computation. (For example, consider the implicit array operations.) What kinds of Fortran statements require non-trivial amounts of computation?

How could the compiler advise the user of the probable complexity of constructions in his program? Would it be worth it? What other aids can you suggest?

6.3 The table of comparisons and exchanges for the three sorts shows that the Shell sort has a much higher ratio of comparisons to exchanges than the interchange sorts. What does this imply? Can the information be used to improve the algorithm?

6.4 Our timing tests of sorting methods were made on arrays of random numbers. Experiment to decide what degree of non-randomness is necessary before the "efficient" sort is faster than the simple sort. What does non-randomness do to the Shell sort?

6.5 Recoding a program in assembly language to make it as fast as possible is a last resort usually taken too early and too often. There is a folk-theorem that "10 per cent of the code takes 90 percent of the run time." Develop a methodology for deciding what parts of a program should be converted to assembly language, based on this observation. (You might try to verify it first.)

6.6 The following program computes prime numbers by the Sieve of Eratosthenes:

```
L=10000;
BEGIN;
DECLARE N(L);
N=1; M=SQRT(L);
DO I=2 TO L;
  IF N(I)=0 THEN GO TO JUMP;
  PUT EDIT (I)(F(5));
  IF I<=M THEN DO K=I TO L/I;
    N(K*I)=0;
  END;
  JUMP:;
END;END;
```

(a) Since two is the only even prime number, modify the program to test only two and odd numbers. (You should clean up the formatting and eliminate the label as you do.) Does your new version run twice as fast as the old? Nearly twice as fast? Measure and see.

(b) Modify the program to save storage by storing only odd numbers in the array N. What effect does this have on the run time?

VII. DOCUMENTATION

The best documentation for a computer program is a clean structure. It also helps if the code is well formatted, with good mnemonic identifiers, labels, and a smattering of enlightening comments. Flowcharts and program descriptions are of secondary importance; the only reliable documentation of a computer program is the code itself. The reason is simple — whenever there are multiple representations of a program, the chance for discrepancy exists. If the code is in error, artistic flowcharts and detailed comments are to no avail.

In Chapter 5 we saw an example where the flowchart said "divide by (n−1)," and the program said

```
VAR = (SUMSQ - (SUMX**2 / AN)) / AN - 1.0
```

The missing parentheses can be detected by doing a few cases by hand and comparing answers, a wise precaution with any program. But the flowchart is of only secondary help — it is right but the code is wrong. Only by reading the code can the programmer know for sure what the program does.

This is not to say that programmers should never write documentation. Quite the contrary. In managing a project of any size it is vital to maintain readable descriptions of what each program is supposed to do, how it is used, how it interacts with other parts of the system, and on what principles it is based. These form useful guides to the code. What is *not* useful is a narrative description of what a given routine actually does on a line-by-line basis. Anything that contributes no new information, but merely echoes the code, is superfluous.

If you wrote your code by first programming in a made up pseudo-language, as we described in Chapter 3, then you already have an excellent "readable description of what each program is supposed to do." Keep the original around to refresh your memory when you have to alter the code — that way you won't have to "decompile" the actual program each time you want to figure out why you did something a certain way. If you put your pseudo-language in as comments at the beginning of your source code, in fact, you will be helping out everyone who must later read it.

Although comments have no effect on code, of course, they are still physically a part of it, and thus provide most of program documentation. We will devote much of our attention to style in commenting.

117

One thing we will *not* do is make pronouncements about how many comments a program should have. We have already seen examples that contain none and others with more comments than program. The right amount usually lies between these extremes, but an arbitrary rule, like "one comment for every three lines," is absurd.

A comment is of zero (or negative) value if it is wrong. For example, in

```
C     TEST FOR NEGATIVE VALUE OF X.
      IF(XST) 5,5,3
      . . .
    5 PRINT 11
   11 FORMAT(1H041HTHE VALUE OF X MUST BE GREATER THAN ZERO.)
```

the comment is certainly not correct, even assuming that X refers to XST. Fortunately this case is sufficiently obvious that it is not likely to mislead.

The more common situation is that the comment, like the flowchart, is correct, but the code it describes is not:

```
/* THIS TIME WE SHALL TEST FOR    */
/* ODD NUMBERS.                    */
IF MOD(X,2)=0 THEN
  DO; SUM = SUM + X;
  ODDNO = ODDNO + 1;
  END;
```

The comment tells us that we are testing for odd numbers, the name ODDNO encourages us to believe it, but the test still selects *even* numbers.

The trouble with comments that do not accurately reflect the code is that they may well be believed subconsciously, so the code itself is not examined critically. A programmer shaky in his understanding of the MOD function might accept this comment at face value, especially since the mnemonic identifier ODDNO provides confirmation. (To avoid this subconscious acceptance, in *The Psychology of Computer Programming* Weinberg suggests that comments should be written on the right side of the page and code on the left, so the comments can be *covered* during debugging.)

Make sure comments and code agree.

Comments should also convey new information:

```
C     NEXT TWO STATEMENTS TEST FOR XMAX, IF LESSTHAN 10**-8,GO TO 1000
C
      EPSI=1.E-8
      IF(XMAX.LE.EPSI) GO TO 1000
```

This contains the same boundary error we saw above — the branch on equality is not what the comment says it is. But even if the comment were true, it would be useless. A meaningful comment would explain the reason for the test instead of merely repeating it in words. Avoid insipid remarks like

```
C     PRINT VALUE OF VOLTAGE
   50 WRITE(6,60) V
```

---

*Don't just echo the code with comments —
make every comment count.*

Comments should help the reader over the difficult spots in a program. But when a comment becomes too involved, we must ask whether the code itself is at fault:

```
      /* WE NEED A LOOP TO PRINT      */
      /* EACH LINE BECAUSE WE ARE     */
      /* PRINTING COLUMNS AS ROWS.    */

      DO J=1 TO 20;

      PUT SKIP EDIT(COL(J),(THRUST(I,J)DO I = 1 TO
           10))(R(FORM));
FORM: FORMAT(X(5),A(9),X(4),10(X(4),F(7,1)));

      /* WE CAN OMIT THE 'END'        */
      /* STATEMENT FOR THIS LOOP      */
      /* BECAUSE WE ARE ABOUT TO END */
      /* THE PROCEDURE.               */
      END CORRECT;
```

The first comment is incorrect, for we can certainly write

```
 PUT EDIT ((COL(J), (THRUST(I,J) DO I = 1 TO 10)
                            DO J = 1 TO 20))
     (SKIP, X(5), A(9), X(4), 10 (X(4), F(7,1)));
```

Since the format FORM appears only once in the program, we have moved it inside the PUT as well, en route adding the right parenthesis missing from the original.

The second comment uses four lines in place of the four characters

```
    END;
```

Should the code be changed, the END will likely have to be added anyway. Indeed the code is explained, probably for pedagogical reasons, but a bad practice well commented remains bad. (The last lines of the maze problem of Chapter 3 contain a similar instance.) A nest of loops should only be terminated by a labeled END when they are short and functionally related, as in

```
INIT: DO I = 1 TO N;
         DO J = 1 TO N;
            X(I,J) = I+J;
      END INIT;
```

Another example where potentially dangerous code is treated with a comment instead of a rewrite is this fragment:

```
   6 E=E+.5
C    TEST FOR VOLTAGE EXCEEDING 3.0.
     IF(E−3.01)5,7,7
```

Since the comment and the code disagree, something is afoot that we are not being told about. Why is the test against 3.01 instead of 3.0? The most likely explanation is that it defends against some form of floating point rounding error, but in the absence of a useful comment, we can only guess. The way to treat this situation is not by adding arbitrary unexplained tolerances to tests. If the code has to be this way, explain it, for it is certainly not obvious. But if (as seems more likely) it reflects a poor algorithm, *change the code.*

Don't comment bad code — rewrite it.

Variable names, labels, and even Fortran statement numbers can aid or hinder documentation. Well-chosen names jog the memory; too-similar or meaningless identifiers hamper understanding. For example:

```
LOGICAL EL,EM,EN,AKK,ELL,EMM,ENN,ELLL,EMMM,ENNN,ELLLL,EMMMM
...
EL = A.EQ.5.*C
EM = B.EQ.A+C
EN = C/B.EQ.C/A
AKK = A/B.EQ.B/C
ELL = A/B.EQ.C
EMM = B.LT.A
ENN = C.GT.B
ELLL = A.GT.C
EMMM = A.GE.B*C
ENNN = EM.OR.EN
ELLLL = EN.AND.AKK
EMMMM = .NOT.(EL.AND.EN)
     PRINT 20,A,B,C,EL,EM,EN,AKK,ELL,EMM,ENN,ELLL,EMMM,ENNN,ELLLL,EMMMM
20   FORMAT (1X,3F10.1,12L5)
```

These names have no mnemonic significance — even AKK, although different from the others for no apparent reason, conveys no information. The similarities invite misunderstanding and typing errors.

One solution might be names reminiscent of the test performed, such as

```
BLTA = B .LT. A
```

but since this seems strained, it is probably easiest to make an array called E and put headings on the output. Then the FORMAT statement can serve as part of the documentation.

Use variable names that mean something.

Statement labels (in PL/I) or numbers (in Fortran) are "mnemonics" just as variable names are — they serve to aid the memory of the person reading the code. Make them meaningful. Look back at the "efficient" sort program of Chapter 6. The sequence of statement labels in it was

```
1, 6, 19, 3, 21, 20, 2, 8, 7, 9, 16, 17
```

When a statement in the middle of the code says

```
GOTO 19
```

which way do you go? Statement labels should be used sparingly (avoid the arithmetic IF, which forces at least two upon you), and should be sequenced in increasing order, with gaps between for later insertions.

Use statement labels that mean something.

The physical layout of a program should also assist the reader (be he the original programmer or later modifier) to understand the logical structure. In Chapter 6 we looked at

```
DECLARE (N,R)FIXED BINARY(31);  ON ENDFILE(SYSIN) GO TO EOJ;
   PUT EDIT('PRIME NUMBER RESULTS')(PAGE,X(13),A);
ST1: GET LIST(N);
   IF N¬>1 THEN
      PUT EDIT('ILLEGAL INPUT N=',N,' <= 1')(SKIP,X(10),A,F(5),A);
   ELSE DO; IF N<=3 THEN GO TO APRIME;
      IF N=2*FLOOR(N/2) THEN  NOPRIME: PUT EDIT(N,' IS NOT A PRIME ',
         'NUMBER')(SKIP,F(15),2 A);
      ELSE DO; DO R=3 TO SQRT(N) BY 2; IF N=R*FLOOR(N/R) THEN
         GO TO NOPRIME; END /* OF DO LOOP */;
APRIME: PUT EDIT(N,' IS A PRIME NUMBER')(SKIP,F(15),A); END; END;
   GO TO ST1;
```

This code follows one layout principle fairly carefully — it is neatly indented to reflect the structure of the conditional statements. However the attempt to squeeze it into only a few lines has made it hard to read, and concealed the convolutions of the code.

Try to find the label NOPRIME, and the executable statement on the same line as a declaration. In the construction

```
IF N¬>1 THEN
   PUT EDIT('ILLEGAL INPUT N=',N,' <= 1')(...)
```

why is the test written differently from the printed output? Separating the semicolon from its statement in

```
END /* OF DO LOOP */;
```

although harmless enough here, is a bad practice to illustrate. Similarly the statement

```
                    PUT EDIT(N,' IS NOT A PRIME ',
   'NUMBER')(SKIP,F(15),2 A);
```

uses the card up to its right boundary to no purpose. The alphabetic string still has to be split onto the next card, which in turn demands the "2 A" format item. Put it all on one line. Our version of this program is in Chapter 6.

Format a program to help the reader understand it.

Another example of how an ill-chosen layout can hinder comprehension is

```
IF  A > B
    THEN S = 1;
    ELSE IF  A = B
        THEN IF  C > D
            THEN S = 2;
            ELSE S = 3;
        ELSE IF  C > D
            THEN S = 4;
            ELSE IF  C = D
                THEN S = 5;
                ELSE S = 6;
```

Again this is neatly indented to display the structure, but it doesn't help the reader to *understand.* Under what circumstances will S be assigned the value three? It is not easy to tell.

If we simply reformat the code:

```
IF          A>B THEN S = 1;
ELSE IF A=B THEN
        IF C>D THEN S = 2;
                ELSE S = 3;
ELSE IF C>D THEN S = 4;
ELSE IF C=D THEN S = 5;
ELSE                S = 6;
```

we can see much more quickly that S is set to three if

$$(A=B) \ \& \ \neg(C>D)$$

The reformatted version reveals that this code is almost in the form of a CASE statement, which we described in Chapter 3. There is one violation: the CASE A=B has an IF–THEN–ELSE in its THEN clause. It is no surprise that this is the hardest part of the code to comprehend. So let us finish the transformation:

```
IF          A>B         THEN S = 1;
ELSE IF A=B & C>D THEN S = 2;
ELSE IF A=B         THEN S = 3;
ELSE IF         C>D THEN S = 4;
ELSE IF         C=D THEN S = 5;
ELSE                        S = 6;
```

At the cost of one additional comparison, we have obtained a familiar structure. Now we know for certain that one, and only one, of the CASEs will be executed. Reading from the top down until the proper condition is met tells us which one.

The reader has undoubtedly noticed by now that our personal stylistic conventions for layout, comments, and the like are not absolutely uniform. If code is clean and simple to begin with, formatting details are of secondary importance.

We conclude with a larger example of documentation. This program solves a set of N linear equations in N unknowns, using Gauss-Seidel elimination. Originally from a textbook, it appeared in an article entitled "How to Write a Readable Fortran Program," in *Datamation*, October, 1972.

```
C CASE STUDY 10
C THE GAUSS-SEIDEL METHOD FOR SOLVING SIMULTANEOUS EQUATIONS
C
C THE PROGRAM SOLVES A SYSTEM OF N EQUATIONS IN N UNKNOWNS.
C N MAY NOT EXCEED 80; N IS READ AS INPUT.
C ONLY THE NON-ZERO ELEMENTS NEED BE ENTERED, ONE ELEMENT PER DATA
C     CARD, WITH ROW AND COLUMN NUMBERS ON EACH CARD.
C A ROW NUMBER OF 99 ACTS AS AN END-OF-DATA SENTINEL.
C THE PROGRAM READS THE FOLLOWING PARAMETERS PRIOR TO ENTERING THE DATA
C     N — THE NUMBER OF EQUATIONS IN THE SYSTEM FOR THIS RUN
C     MAXIT — THE MAXIMUM NUMBER OF ITERATIONS TO BE PERMITTED
C     EPSLON — THE CONVERGENCE CRITERION
C     BIGGST — THE MAXIMUM SIZE (IN ABSOLUTE VALUE) TO BE PERMITTED
C         OF ANY COEFFICIENT OR CONSTANT TERM
C ALL INPUT IS CHECKED FOR VALIDITY, EVEN IF AN ERROR IS FOUND.
C
C
        DIMENSION A(80, 81), X(80)
        LOGICAL OK
C
C CLEAR ARRAYS
        DO 20 I = 1, 80
          X(I) = 0.0
          DO 10 J = 1, 81
            A(I, J) = 0.0
   10     CONTINUE
   20   CONTINUE
C
C READ CONTROL PARAMETERS DESCRIBED IN INTRODUCTORY COMMENTS
        READ (5, 100) N, MAXIT, EPSLON, BIGGST
        NPLUS1 = N + 1
C
C READ THE ELEMENTS OF THE ARRAYS, WITH CHECKING
C DO LOOP IS USED TO CONTROL MAXIMUM NUMBER OF ELEMENTS
C FIRST SET ERROR COUNT TO ZERO
        NERROR = 0
        LIMIT = N*NPLUS1 + 1
        DO 30 K = 1, LIMIT
          READ (5, 100) I, J, TEMP
          IF ( I .EQ. 99 ) GO TO 41
          OK = .TRUE.
          IF (      (I .LT. 1)
     1        .OR. (I .GT. N)
     2        .OR. (J .LT. 1)
     3        .OR. (J .GT. NPLUS1)
     4        .OR. (ABS(TEMP) .GT. BIGGST) ) OK = .FALSE.
          IF (      OK ) A(I, J) = TEMP
          IF ( .NOT. OK ) WRITE (6, 110) I, J, TEMP
          IF ( .NOT. OK ) NERROR = NERROR + 1
   30   CONTINUE
```

continued on next page

```
C
C IF DO IS SATISFIED, THERE WERE TOO MANY DATA CARDS FOR THE
C    VALUE OF N THAT WAS SPECIFIED — WRITE ERROR COMMENT
         WRITE (6, 120)
         STOP
C
C ALL DATA CARDS HAVE BEEN READ — CHECK ERROR COUNT AND STOP IF ANY
     41  IF ( NERROR .NE. 0 ) WRITE ( 6, 130) NERROR
         IF ( NERROR .NE. 0 ) STOP
C
C        BEGIN ITERATION SCHEME — DO LOOP COUNTS THE NUMBER OF ITERATIONS
         DO 70 ITER = 1, MAXIT
C
C            ... NEXT STATEMENT IS EXECUTED ONCE PER SWEEP OF THE SYSTEM
             RESID = 0.0
C
C            ... INDEX I SELECTS A ROW
             DO 60 I = 1, N
C
C                ... NEXT STATEMENT IS EXECUTED ONCE PER ROW
                 SUM = 0.0
C
C                ... GET SUM OF TERMS IN ROW I, NOT INCLUDING DIAGONAL TERM
                 DO 50 J = 1, N
                     IF ( J .NE. I ) SUM = SUM + A(I,J)*X(J)
     50          CONTINUE
C
C                ... COMPUTE THE NEW APPROXIMATION TO VARIABLE X(I)
                 TEMP = (A(I, NPLUS1) — SUM) / A(I,I)
C
C                ... AT THE END OF A SWEEP OF ALL EQUATIONS, THE FOLLOWING
C                ... STATEMENT WILL HAVE PUT LARGEST RESIDUAL IN RESID
                 IF (ABS(TEMP — X(I)) .GT. RESID ) RESID = ABS(TEMP — X(I))
C
C                ... STORE NEW APPROXIMATION TO VARIABLE X(I)
                 X(I) = TEMP
     60      CONTINUE
C
C            ... ONE SWEEP HAS NOW BEEN COMPLETED —  PRINT VARIABLES
             WRITE (6, 140) (X(K), K = 1, N)
C
C            ... IF LARGEST RESIDUAL LESS THAN EPSLON, PROCESS HAS CONVERGED
             IF ( RESID .LT. EPSLON ) STOP
     70  CONTINUE
C
C IF THIS OUTER DO IS EVER SATISFIED, MORE THAN MAXIT ITERATIONS WOULD
C    BE NEEDED FOR CONVERGENCE — WRITE ERROR COMMENT AND GIVE UP
         WRITE (6, 150) MAXIT
         STOP
C
C
    100  FORMAT (2I2, 2F10.0)
    110  FORMAT (1X, 'ERROR IN CARD WITH I = ',I2,', J = ',I2,
        1    ', VALUE = ', 1PE14.6)
    120  FORMAT ('0', 'DECK CONTAINED TOO MANY CARDS')
    130  FORMAT ('0', 'ERRORS FOUND IN ', I4, ' DATA CARDS — JOB ABORTED')
    140  FORMAT ('0', 8F12.5)
    150  FORMAT ('0', 'PROCESS DID NOT CONVERGE IN', I4, ' ITERATIONS')
         END
```

In many ways, this is an excellent program. It validates its input data. It uses, instead of abusing, the idea of falling out of the bottom of a DO loop when one should not. In several places, the authors have sacrificed a tiny amount of computation time by re-testing a condition, to avoid extra labels and GOTOs.

And it is thoroughly commented and neatly formatted. Notice that even the data is commented. One of the most effective ways to document a program is simply to describe the data layout in detail. If you can specify for each important variable what values it can assume and how it gets changed, you have gone a long way to describing the program. (The checker-playing subroutine we looked at in Chapter 3 is another good example.)

Document your data layouts.

All in all, the code above is a model of programming style.

But there are a few difficulties. To begin with, what about modularity? When a single routine sprawls over several pages, it is hard to follow. Since well over half of the actual code is concerned with validating the data, this could profitably be made a separate input subroutine. Then the main program could read

```
CALL INPUT(N, A, MAXIT, EPSLON, OK)
IF (.NOT. OK) STOP
```

The modularization would have the advantage that each part of the program would fit comfortably on one page. (In fairness, we should observe that the textbook from which this program originally came had not yet introduced subroutines before the example was presented.)

And what about its readability? Here is a letter to the editor of *Datamation*, published shortly after the original article.

> In the October issue, [...] told us "How to Write a Readable Fortran Program." I wish they had followed their own advice in the example that they gave. Said example has so many comments in it that it is unreadable. I agree that program documentation is a long-neglected and important problem. And placing a comment card before each statement in a program *does* document it. It also makes the program unreadable. Grouping Fortran comments and program statements into logical blocks makes *both* of them readable with very little loss of clarity.
>
> Neal Paris
> Durham, North Carolina

Mr. Paris has a point. There are more comments than program; some of them convey little information.

Don't over-comment.

A second letter on the same subject also appeared in *Datamation:*

> The example given in the article, "How to Write a
> Readable Fortran Program" (Oct., p 73), illustrates one of
> the most common faults of comments in programs —
> that the comments don't agree with the program. The
> program itself illustrates one of the commonest program-
> ming mistakes — the failure to check controlling parame-
> ters for limits.
>
> Specifically, the last line of comment in the heading
> states reassuringly: "All input is checked for validity." So
> what happens? The very first READ statement reads four
> controlling parameters which are checked only by the
> field width in the format, not a very good way to do it.
> In particular, N is not checked for its limit of 80. The un-
> checked N is used to "check" the values of I and J.
> Hence, a too-large N may result in storing of data beyond
> the array bounds. The unchecked N also limits several
> DO loops in the program.
>
> N. M. Taylor
> Washington, D.C.

Mr. Taylor is also right. The comment, like the input checking, is slightly
wrong.

As a final observation, not worth a letter to *Datamation,* try the program on
the equations

$$Y = 1.0$$
$$X + Y = 2.0$$

The solution is obviously X=1.0, Y=1.0. What does the program do? Following
the code, when I equals one in the first pass through the inner loop, we evaluate
(one line after statement 50)

```
TEMP = (A(I, NPLUS1) - SUM) / A(I,I)
```

What is A(I,I) when I is one? It is the coefficient of X in the first equation.
What is the coefficient of X in the first equation? Zero. What is the result of
dividing by zero? Disaster.

The program, comments and formatting notwithstanding, fails on a
significant class of equations — those which happen to have or develop a zero
on the diagonal. And it little matters how "readable" a program is if it does not
work. (Of course, those familiar with the limitations of Gauss-Seidel elimination would know enough to avoid such cases, and the textbook contains a proper warning.) Perhaps what the article really shows is that people who attempt

to criticize programming style run the risk of being criticized in turn. On that note we bring our discussion to a close.

In summary:

(1) If a program is incorrect, it matters little what the documentation says.

(2) If documentation does not agree with the code, it is not worth much.

(3) Consequently, code must largely document itself. If it cannot, rewrite the code rather than increase the supplementary documentation. Good code needs fewer comments than bad code does.

(4) Comments should provide additional information that is not readily obtainable from the code itself. They should never parrot the code.

(5) Mnemonic variable names and labels, and a layout that emphasizes logical structure, help make a program self-documenting.

POINTS TO PONDER

7.1 Programming in a standard or stereotyped way is often a useful way to avoid error. For example, in Fortran, identifiers that begin with I, J, K, L, M, or N are integer by default, and all others are floating point. This convention is widely used.

Sometimes, however, to avoid straining for meaningful identifiers, it seems easier to declare variables explicitly, overriding the default. From the standpoints of error potential and reader comprehension, is this good practice or bad? You might consider this excerpt in your deliberations:

```
C A SORTING PROGRAM
      ...
      INTEGER X, Y
      DIMENSION X(25), Y(25)
      ...
            IF ( X(I) .LE. X(J) ) GO TO 20
                TEMP = X(I)
                X(I) = X(J)
                X(J) = TEMP
                TEMP = Y(I)
                Y(I) = Y(J)
                Y(J) = TEMP
```

7.2 Fortran continuation cards are often left behind when statements are moved in a program deck. What practices can you think of, in writing multi-line statements, that would reduce the likelihood of your making this mistake (or at least ensure that the compiler will spot your error)? Look back over the Fortran programs in this book.

7.3 Comment on these comments:

```
      DO 65 L=1,9999
C         GENERATE RANDOM NUMBER
41    CALL RANDU(IX,IY,YFL)
C         SET NEW VALUE OF IX TO VALUE OF IY
      IX=IY
C         COMPUTE SAMPLE WHICH IS TO RECEIVE BACTERIA
      N=YFL*100.0 +1.0
C         CHECK TO SEE IF N IS 101
      IF(N-101) 40,41,40
C         CHECK TO SEE IF SAMPLE ALREADY CONTAINS BACTERIA
40    IF(IT(N) )21,20,21
C         INCREMENT NUMBER OF SAMPLES CONTAINING BACTERIA BY ONE
20    ICT=ICT+1
C         INCREMENT NUMBER OF BACTERIA IN SAMPLE BY ONE
21    IT(N)=IT(N)+1
C         CHECK TO SEE IF 50 OF THE SAMPLES CONTAIN BACTERIA
      IF(ICT-50)65,33,33
65    CONTINUE
```

EPILOGUE

It is time to take stock. Although we have touched on many aspects of computer programming in the last seven chapters, much has been left unsaid. In some cases this was due to lack of space, but most of the omissions were intentional. There are many good books on languages, algorithms and numerical methods available to those who want to learn programming in greater depth. Our goal was not to teach languages or algorithms, but to teach you to program well.

Programmers have a strong tendency to underrate the importance of good style. Eternally optimistic, we all like to think that once we throw a piece of code together, however haphazardly, it will work properly the first time and ever after. Why waste time cleaning up something that is almost certain to be correct? Besides, it probably will be used for only a few weeks.

There are really two answers to the question. The first is suggested by the word "almost." A slap-dash piece of code that falls short of perfection can be a difficult creature to deal with. The self-discipline of writing it cleanly the first time increases your chances of getting it right and eases the task of fixing it if it is not. The programmer who leaps to the coding pad and throws his first draft at the machine spends far more of his life redoing and debugging than does his more careful brother.

The second point is that phrase "only a few weeks." Certainly we write code differently depending on the ultimate use we expect to make of it. But computer centers are full of programs that were written for a short-term use, then were pressed into years of service. Not only pressed, but sometimes hammered and twisted. It is often simpler to modify existing code, no matter how badly written, than to reinvent the wheel yet again for a new application. Big programs — operating systems, compilers, major applications — are never written to be used once and discarded. They change and evolve. Most professional programmers spend much of their time *changing* other people's code. We will say it once more — clean code is easier to maintain.

One excuse for writing an unintelligible program is that it is a private matter. Only the original programmer will ever look at it, and surely he need not spell out everything when he has it all in his head. This can be a strong argument, particularly if you don't program professionally. It is the same justification you use for writing "qt milk, fish, big box" for a grocery list instead of composing a proper sentence. If the list is intended for someone else, of

131

course, you had better specify what kind of fish you want and what should be inside that big box. But even if only you personally want to understand the message, if it is to be readable a year from now you must write a complete sentence. So in your diary you might write, "Today I went to the supermarket and bought a quart of milk, a pound of halibut, and a big box of raisins."

You learn to write as if to someone else because *next year you will be "someone else."* Schools teach English composition, not how to write grocery lists. The latter is easy once the former is mastered. Yet when it comes to computer programming, many programmers seem to think that a mastery of "grocery list" writing is adequate preparation for composing large programs. This is not so.

The essence of what we are trying to convey is summed up in the elusive word "style." It is not a list of rules so much as an approach and an attitude. "Good programmers" are those who already have learned a set of rules that ensures good style; many of them will read this book and see no reason to change. If you are still learning to be a "good programmer," however, then perhaps some of what we consider good style will have rubbed off in the reading.

SUPPLEMENTARY READING

D. W. Barron, *Recursive Techniques in Programming*. American Elsevier, 1968.

W. Strunk, Jr., and E. B. White, *The Elements of Style*. MacMillan, 1972.

G. M. Weinberg, *The Psychology of Computer Programming*. Van Nostrand Reinhold, 1971.

SUMMARY OF RULES

This summary is designed to give a quick review of the points we covered in the book. Remember as you read the rules that they were presented in connection with one or more examples — go back and reread the pertinent section if a rule doesn't call them to mind.

To paraphrase an observation in *The Elements of Style,* rules of programming style, like those of English, are sometimes broken, even by the best writers. When a rule is broken, however, you will usually find in the program some compensating merit, attained at the cost of the violation. Unless you are certain of doing as well, you will probably do best to follow the rules.

Write clearly — don't be too clever.

Say what you mean, simply and directly.

Use library functions.

Avoid temporary variables.

Write clearly — don't sacrifice clarity for "efficiency."

Let the machine do the dirty work.

Replace repetitive expressions by calls to a common function.

Parenthesize to avoid ambiguity.

Choose variable names that won't be confused.

Avoid the Fortran arithmetic IF.

Avoid unnecessary branches.

Don't use conditional branches as a substitute for a logical expression.

If a logical expression is hard to understand, try transforming it.

Use data arrays to avoid repetitive control sequences.

Choose a data representation that makes the program simple.

Write first in an easy-to-understand pseudo-language; then translate into whatever language you have to use.

Use IF...ELSE IF...ELSE IF...ELSE... to implement multi-way branches.

Modularize. Use subroutines.

Use GOTOs only to implement a fundamental structure.

Avoid GOTOs completely if you can keep the program readable.

Don't patch bad code — rewrite it.

Write and test a big program in small pieces.

Use recursive procedures for recursively-defined data structures.

Test input for plausibility and validity.

Make sure input doesn't violate the limits of the program.

Terminate input by end-of-file or marker, not by count.

Identify bad input; recover if possible.

Make input easy to prepare and output self-explanatory.

Use uniform input formats.

Make input easy to proofread.

Use free-form input when possible.

Use self-identifying input. Allow defaults. Echo both on output.

Make sure all variables are initialized before use.

Don't stop at one bug.

Use debugging compilers.

Initialize constants with DATA statements or INITIAL attributes; initialize variables with executable code.

Watch out for off-by-one errors.

Take care to branch the right way on equality.

Be careful when a loop exits to the same place from side and bottom.

Make sure your code "does nothing" gracefully.

Test programs at their boundary values.

Check some answers by hand.

10.0 times 0.1 is hardly ever 1.0.

Don't compare floating point numbers solely for equality.

Make it right before you make it faster.

Make it fail-safe before you make it faster.

Make it clear before you make it faster.

Don't sacrifice clarity for small gains in "efficiency."

Let your compiler do the simple optimizations.

Don't strain to re-use code; reorganize instead.

Make sure special cases are truly special.

Keep it simple to make it faster.

Don't diddle code to make it faster — find a better algorithm.

Instrument your programs. Measure before making "efficiency" changes.

Make sure comments and code agree.

Don't just echo the code with comments — make every comment count.

Don't comment bad code — rewrite it.

Use variable names that mean something.

Use statement labels that mean something.

Format a program to help the reader understand it.

Document your data layouts.

Don't over-comment.

INDEX

variance, computing a, 90

WATFIV compiler, 62, 81
WATFOR compiler, 62, 81
ways to reach a statement, 18, 19, 40, 43, 45
Weinberg, G.M., viii, 118, 133
WHILE statement, 45
White, E.B., viii, 133
White Rabbit, 44
wrong way on equality, branching, 84, 85, 94, 118, 119

zero times, DO loop done, 55, 88, 94, 106
zero, division by, 4, 7, 9, 14, 127